THE SEVEN STRENGTHS OF SUMMITING

SUMMITING YOUR FIRST BIG MOUNTAIN

BY MARK SANTINO
EDITED BY MARIA LATHAM

The Seven Strengths of Summiting | **Mark Santino**

This publication is designed to provide competent and reliable information regarding the subject matter covered. However, it is sold with the understanding that the author and publisher are not engaged in furnishing medical, scientific, or other professional advice. Laws and practices often vary from state to state, and country to country, and if expert assistance is required, the services of a professional should be sought. The author and publisher specifically disclaim any liability that is incurred from the use or application of the contents of this book. Hiking, trekking, climbing, adventure travel and related activities are inherently dangerous. The reader should have the utmost respect for the power and volatility of nature and assumes all associated risk. The reader should consult with a physician before undergoing intensely strenuous physical activity at any altitude. Every effort has been made to provide accurate information and website addresses at the time of publication; neither the author nor the publisher assumes any responsibilities for changes that occur after publishing. While many product names are referenced in this book, the author does not receive any compensation from the manufacturers for their reference.

The Seven Strengths of Summiting: Summiting Your First Big Mountain
First Edition: February 2020
ISBN: 979-8615454332
Copyright © 2020 by Mark Santino

All Rights Reserved. No part of this publication may be reproduced, stored in a retrieval system or transmitted in any form by any means, electronic, mechanical, photocopying, recording or otherwise, except brief extracts for the purpose of review, without the written permission of the author.

Photographs courtesy of the following: Mark Santino, John Santino, Ivett Santino, Shawn Burton, Doug Goldstein, Christopher Blogg, Cosmin Ioan, and Jeff Davidson.

Follow us at: INSTAGRAM: @SevenStrengthsOfSummiting
                 FACEBOOK: facebook.com/SevenStrengthsOfSummiting/

The Seven Strengths of Summiting | **Mark Santino**

DEDICATION

....

*"Families are the compass that guides us.
They are the inspiration to reach great heights,
and our comfort when we occasionally falter."
– Brad Henry*

The Seven Strengths of Summiting | **Mark Santino**

This book is dedicated to my wife Ivett and our two children, Nicole and Joey, and our extended family. You have always supported my thrilling and time-consuming hobby, holding down the fort in my absence while spending endless nights waiting for an update when I was in extremely remote locations with no connectivity to the outside world. Every day I was away, you were constantly on my mind. The thought of being back home with you was my inspiration to push through the challenges and be cautious in my decisions made in the mountains. I love you!

I also dedicate this book to my many climbing partners, guides, and porters across the globe over the years. Thank you for the friendship and sharing the passion and the adventures with me — pushing me when I needed to be pushed, helping me see the beauty along the way, and ensuring I got home safely!

TABLE OF CONTENTS

WELCOME TO THE MOUNTAINS!	1
INTRODUCING THE SEVEN STRENGTHS	5
STRENGTH #1: Physical Strength	9
STRENGTH #2: Cardiovascular Strength	21
STRENGTH #3: Altitudinal Strength	27
STRENGTH #4: Mental, Emotional, and Spiritual Strength	39
STRENGTH #5: Team Strength	49
STRENGTH #6: Preparation Strength	57
STRENGTH #7: Gear Strength	69
SAMPLE GEAR LIST	95
THE JOURNEY IS THE DESTINATION	101
CONCLUSION	109
BONUS CHAPTER: The Seven Strengths of Summiting in Business	113
RECOMMENDED READING	117
APPENDICES	119
APPENDIX A: Mount Whitney (1997)	121
APPENDIX B: Mount Everest Base Camp (2004)	133
APPENDIX C: Mount Kilimanjaro (2007)	163
ABOUT THE AUTHOR	199

The Seven Strengths of Summiting | **Mark Santino**

The Seven Strengths of Summiting | **Mark Santino**

WELCOME TO THE MOUNTAINS!

....

*"Of all the paths you take in life,
make sure a few of them are dirt."
– John Muir*

The Seven Strengths of Summiting | **Mark Santino**

This book is written for the average Joe / average Jane who is looking for some insights on what another average Joe did to prepare for ascending some of the most formidable mountains on the planet.

If you're a new hiker just starting out, my advice is to start small and work your way up. Initially, try hiking a smaller mountain requiring just a day hike up and back, in good weather. Over time, work your way up to larger treks that span multiple days and nights, on terrain that is physically demanding and requires altitude acclimatization, and with weather that's far from perfect. Be aware that this acclimatization process involves both your mental and physical states. If you take the time to gradually expose yourself to bigger challenges in the mountains, you'll build the experience base to answer the demands, and begin to get comfortable with being uncomfortable.

I strongly recommend that you don't view the summit as the ultimate objective. It's really only the halfway point; you also need to make it back home safely for the summit to 'count'. Any physical and mental preparations you make in advance of the climb and during your days in the mountains should be with this in mind at all times. And if you adopt a perspective that the journey is the destination, even if you can't make it to the physical summit due to foul weather, lack of daylight, exhaustion, etc., it will be a successful adventure regardless.

You may see the terms *hiking, trekking, backpacking, mountaineering, climbing,* and *summiting* used interchangeably throughout this book.

While there are distinctions between these, each involves the Seven Strengths.

- **Hiking** refers to walking on a trail, usually in the woods or wilderness.

- **Backpacking** is hiking for multiple days and nights, while wearing a backpack to carry gear such as a tent, a sleeping bag, etc.

- **Trekking** is a term commonly used to describe a more challenging combination of both of these activities, and is frequently used outside of the U.S. (In New Zealand, it is known as *tramping*, and the military commonly uses the term *rucking*).

- **Climbing** might suggest vertical rock climbing with ropes, harnesses, and anchors, although many hikes require some scrambling which might be referred to as climbing (for example, the Knife Edge route on Mount Katahdin, Angels Landing in Zion National Park, or the Barranco Wall on Mount Kilimanjaro).

- **Mountaineering** typically involves alpine climbing on snow and ice requiring gear such as crampons, ice axes, ropes, etc., as would be needed to summit Mount Shasta.

- **Summiting** is the act of reaching the summit of a peak on the trail, although some hikes won't really hit a true summit (for example, the Inca Trail or the Teton Crest Trail).

As an aside, my trekking partners and I have observed that not a lot of folks that we interact with daily (family, co-workers, neighbors, etc.) are particularly interested in having mountain adventures like those covered in this book. In this modern era of competing life priorities, digital overload, and working round the clock, the reality is that outdoor adventure may be uncomfortable and hard work, it may be potentially expensive, and the time away may place a strain on family or work obligations. While it's understandable that mountain adventures may not be for everyone, with preparation I hope that all do get a chance to experience what they've been missing out on!

The Seven Strengths of Summiting | **Mark Santino**

INTRODUCING THE SEVEN STRENGTHS

"Adventuring can be for the ordinary person with ordinary qualities, such as I regard myself."
– Sir Edmund Hillary

When I was a little more than a year old, my parents took the family camping. Our camp wasn't perched at 14,000 feet with gale-force winds blasting the tent but look at the smile on my face – clearly, I was hooked from the very beginning! And, thank you, Mom and Dad, for exposing us to the great outdoors!

In high school, my buddies and I would head deep into the woods or boat out to an island to camp. It was pretty obvious that we knew nothing about how to do it properly. Forget about traveling light: I'd lug a huge metal cooler containing bacon and eggs, ice and other essentials, a cast iron skillet, plus a massive cotton sleeping bag that must've weighed at least eight pounds.

Years later, I moved to Tucson, Arizona, and discovered the Outdoor Adventures program at the University of Arizona. I dove into spelunking, rock climbing, mountain biking, and hiking/trekking, and with the benefit of great instruction from knowledgeable experts, I started to learn the *right* way to do it.

From that point on, I focused on mountain biking and hiking the multiple mountain ranges and valleys throughout Arizona. Five years later, I moved out to Northern California for work, and found a couple of like-minded buddies to share my adventures with. The rest is history.

When you're in your early twenties, the primary strength you tend to rely on is physical strength. I focused on strength training at the gym and in my garage, and at the time I avoided cardio, which I thought was too hard. As I gained more experience, learning to be safe and confident summiting mountains throughout the United States and around the globe, I realized that getting to the top actually requires seven different, yet complementary strengths, not just one.

The Seven Strengths of Summiting are:
- Physical Strength
- Cardiovascular Strength
- Altitudinal Strength
- Mental, Emotional, and Spiritual Strength
- Team Strength
- Preparation Strength
- Gear Strength

The strengths, I have learned, are all interconnected, and in most cases, one strength relies on another. For example, the strong leg muscles (**physical**) that you will gain from your **cardiovascular** training on a Stairmaster or exercise bike will absolutely enhance your endurance in climbing and descending high altitude terrain. If you've got thick skin and are resilient (**mental**), while in a challenging section of the climb with your **team**, you can support and encourage the others to push through their self-doubt and motivate them to continue to ascend to the next camp. If you've got all the lightest high-tech **gear** but don't research (**preparation**) the micro-climates you'll be traversing through, you can find yourself having to turn back when a coastal squall comes in without notice and hammers the trekking party.

The main chapters of the book are focused on these Seven Strengths. In addition, there are appendices in the form of trekking logs from three notable treks, which is where the Seven Strengths – the foundation of this book – were born.

Disclaimer: Hiking, trekking, climbing and adventure travel are inherently dangerous. The reader should have the utmost respect for the power and volatility of nature and assumes all associated risk. The reader should consult with a physician before partaking in intensely strenuous physical activity at any altitude.

STRENGTH #1:
PHYSICAL STRENGTH

....

"What we face may look insurmountable. But I learned something from all those years of training and competing. I learned something from all those sets and reps when I didn't think I could lift another ounce of weight. What I learned is that we are always stronger than we know."
– Arnold Schwarzenegger

When climbing your first big mountain, being physically strong is essential. But muscular strength alone is not enough to guarantee success. An iron constitution and the proper balance of hygiene and nutrition are needed to stay healthy and battle through exhaustion – this constant struggle is ever-present trekking at high altitude.

Muscular Strength – When we hear someone talking about "strength", we automatically think of physical (muscular) strength. To carry a 50-plus-pound backpack up near-vertical trails in the Himalayas, or to undertake a winter ascent where backpack weights can reach 70 pounds or more while traversing across thigh-height snow, you need to have a strong core, shoulders, back, and legs. There's no doubt that mountain trekking is physically hard work and being physically strong is important to keep moving up the mountain to your destination, and back down to safety.

My typical routine to prepare my legs for the ascent and descent looks something like this:

(1) Stairmaster – I begin my workout with the Stairmaster to warm up my muscles and get the blood flowing. When I start training (several months before the climb), I warm up with a 5-minute session set to a mid-difficulty level. By the time I'm approaching the final few weeks before the climb, I'm usually doing 15-20 minutes, sprinting at the maximum difficulty level.

(2) Leg press – I sometimes interchange this with squats; however, the leg press machine provides more control and safety for my bad knees. I usually do 3-4 sets with moderate weight.

(3) Quad extensions and quad curls – I super-set these, doing a set of 10 extensions followed by 10 curls without rest between the extensions and the curls. I do 3-4 sets of both. This no-rest super-setting has a cardio benefit as well.

(4) Box jumps, wall sits, crunches and planks are also great for your legs and core strength.

(5) Mountain biking – I recommend terrain with some aggressive uphill sections to really strengthen the legs. If your bike has pedals with clips, instead of only pushing on the downstroke, try pulling on the upstroke as well. This challenges a different set of leg muscles, and I have found it increases stamina. Mountain biking is also an excellent cardio workout.

(6) Local hiking – Nothing can prepare you better for trekking in the mountains than doing frequent local hikes with a loaded pack before you head to the mountain destination. If you can, hike in a variety of weather conditions to see how you and your gear handle it. Ideally, you'll be climbing taller mountains locally to help with altitude preparation. And, don't forget to wear the boots and clothes you plan on wearing in the mountains to break them in.

(7) Weighted vest – Doing any of these exercises with a 20-pound (or 40-pound) weighted vest will accelerate your training and increase your physical strength.

It is important to note that the leg muscles used in climbing up mountains are not exactly the same as the muscles used in descent. For example, I find that the area where the quadriceps connect on the inside of the leg near the knee (called the Vastus Medialis) gets fatigued on descent. If the only conditioning you do is on is Stairmaster, which strengthens the leg muscles used for climbing, you will be surprised at how sore and tired you will get coming down the mountain.

The descent also puts a lot of strain on the knees. Because I've had knee (ACL and Medial Meniscus) surgeries, I make sure my legs are trained to be strong going up *and* coming down. Using trekking poles will alleviate some of the descent strain, but nothing beats proper conditioning, as I realized on Mount Kilimanjaro:

> *The scree descent was a nightmare. This is where accidents happen – altitude, tired muscles, exhaustion, and loose dirt/rocks. We learned from Cos that he was so bad off from the cerebral edema, he slid all the way down the scree on his butt, tearing up his Gore-Tex pants and his bottom side. Kirsten's knee was killing her. Julius took her pack and she descended very slowly. I went slowly too – my legs were tired and getting*

more tired with every second, trying to protect my knees by breaking with my quads.

Ability to Battle Through Exhaustion and Fatigue — It is rare that I get a good night's rest in the mountains. Trekking 10 or more miles in a day with a full pack is physically exhausting, so you'd expect to pass out as soon as you lie down at night. However, all too often the high elevations equal poor sleep as your body struggles to pull enough oxygen out of the thin air. The combination of exhaustion, thin air, and subpar sleeping surfaces (for some reason I can feel every rock underneath me!) makes it very difficult to sleep, and it's not uncommon to be kept awake from the noise of the weather outside the tent or your tent-mate's snoring (or even worse, being jolted awake by the sound of your own snoring!).

There's the added challenge of animals rummaging outside the tent at night. My wife and I had a bear encounter at Yosemite, and I can tell you that in those circumstances, just hearing the cracking of a twig in the woods and movement in the distance will keep you up all night.

At popular locations such as Mount Everest Base Camp, the noise from other trekking parties can interfere with your sleep. So can the unfortunate outcome of another trekking party's decision to eat yak meat at a tea house on the way up to Mount Everest Base Camp. Listening to them racing back and forth to the facilities with diarrhea and vomiting all is brutal! (True story.)

At altitude, "Things That Keep You Awake At Night" also may include wondering if your tent will get torn to shreds by the high winds whipping around outside the flaps; praying water stays out of the tent during torrential rainfalls; listening to the thunder clap violently nearby while lightning lights up your tent all night, and praying it doesn't hit your metal tent poles; or being soothed by the silence of gently falling snow, but growing increasingly concerned that as it piles up, it will collapse the tent poles of your tent or cover up your tent's ventilation port, which is busily keeping you alive with the proper mix of oxygen and carbon dioxide.

The list could also include the sound of rescue helicopters evacuating trekkers every few hours during the night in the Khumbu Valley on the Everest Base Camp trek. Even the anticipation of the next day's summit or beautiful vista will keep your mind racing all night!

But if you're summiting the next day on a big mountain, you will need to wake up at "0-Dark-Thirty" (midnight or 1:00 am, or as early as 10:00 pm in the case of Mount Kilimanjaro). This is called an "alpine start," which has you climbing through the night to reach the summit in the morning.

There are a few reasons for this. First, it keeps you off the exposed section of the mountain by the time those volatile afternoon storms arrive. Second, snow and ice are more stable when frozen, and the alpine start keeps you away from dangerous conditions that can occur as the day progresses and the sun begins to thaw the ground cover.

Lastly, the early start gives you enough time to summit, return to base camp, pack up everything, and get to the evening's camp (or off the mountain), while there's still daylight.

An alpine start does have its drawbacks, however. For example, you'll be climbing in a state of exhaustion after struggling with little sleep at altitude during the nights leading up to the summit attempt. You'll also miss out on the visual experience of the ascent, and as it's nearly impossible to recognize landscape features in the darkness, it's a challenge to avoid hazards on the ascent and know where you've been if a rapid decent is needed.

Sleep is critical if your body is to recover from the beating it's taking, but as I've mentioned, deep, restorative sleep is elusive at altitude. Not only is pushing yourself forward very difficult with this inadequate rest, but clear thinking and decision-making falter as well.

Iron Constitution – Having an iron constitution (i.e. resisting getting sick) is also essential. Traveling to countries with water sources containing bacteria you're unaccustomed to often brings on a case of traveler's diarrhea.

When we were acclimatizing for our Inca Trail trek in and around Cusco, I got sick from the food or the water, or both. Because dehydration from diarrhea is common – and to avoid my adventure ending before it even began – I started an antibiotics regimen. By the time I finished the antibiotics, I was feeling great again and we were being shuttled to the Salcantay trail head. A couple of days into our trek to Machu Picchu, by way of the Salcantay route to the Inca Trail, I got sick again. Whether it was a food-borne illness from poor meal prep on the trail, or water that hadn't been boiled long enough, I had my second bout of diarrhea in two weeks.

Water-Borne and Food-Borne Bacteria – Water comes to a boil faster at altitude. The general rule of thumb is that for every 1000 feet of elevation, the boiling point drops by 2 degrees Fahrenheit, so while water normally boils at 212 degrees Fahrenheit/100 degrees Celsius at your home at sea level, at 10,000 feet it comes to a boil at 192 degrees Fahrenheit (89 degrees Celsius). At this lower boiling temperature, it's advised to boil water a bit longer than usual to kill any bacteria that may be present in the water source.

- https://www.fsis.usda.gov/shared/PDF/High_Altitude_Cooking_and_Food_Safety.pdf

The EPA recommends boiling water for three minutes versus the normal one minute at altitudes over 5,000 feet.

- https://www.epa.gov/ground-water-and-drinking-water/emergency-disinfection-drinking-water

Be very aware of *all* the water you're intaking, not just what you drink. Many novice trekkers are hyper-aware of the purity of their drinking water, but fail to consider the purity of the water for (a) washing their face, (b) cleaning their hands to put in contact lenses, (c) putting on their toothbrush, or (d) the ice cubes in their drink at the restaurant en route to the trail head. Depending on your level of sensitivity, the cleanliness of the water source and the quality of food preparation, you may need to be concerned about eating fresh produce in local restaurants overseas and in the high-altitude lodges you might find on your mountain trek.

I always use UV Light Purifier Pens (like Steripen), water purification tablets, and/or water filters to ensure the water I drink is safe. If you're concerned about food preparation and food-borne bacteria, ensure all food is cooked thoroughly, avoid eating meat in the mountains, and if you're really worried, bring your own freeze-dried food and energy bars.

Hygiene — It's worth the extra effort to wash your hands with soap frequently, use baby wipes to keep clean, and make liberal use of hand sanitizer to stay healthy as you travel to your adventure destination, and while on the trek itself.

If you're on a flight with a lot of coughing passengers on the way out to your foreign mountain destination, put your ego aside and throw on a N95-rated mask to help keep the bacteria away. When SARS broke out in Asia several years back, I wore a N95 mask and used plenty of hand sanitizer and took the opportunity to see Angkor Wat, Cambodia while the flights were cheap and nearly empty due to the outbreak.

Inoculations – Americans traveling to remote wilderness locations overseas should have the appropriate inoculations recommended by the U.S. Center for Disease Control:
- https://wwwnc.cdc.gov/travel

(Trekkers from other countries should follow their national guidelines.)

Note that some inoculations may have unpleasant side effects. Due to the large number of rabid dogs in Kathmandu and in the Nepalese Himalayas, it is advised to get three doses of rabies vaccinations. I took my last dose a few days before the trek to Mount Everest Base Camp began and got slammed by side effects that included high fever, cold sweats, and dizziness. It nearly derailed the climb, but fortunately, the symptoms cleared the morning of the departure from Kathmandu and flight to Lukla, where the trek began.

The few times I took antimalarial pills, the side effects (anxiety, vivid (crazy!) dreams, nausea, vomiting, abdominal pain, and diarrhea), scared the crap out of me, but I went the prudent route, took the prescribed dosage, and fared okay.

Nutrition – While we all love great-tasting food, in preparation for trekking and while the mountains, food should be viewed strictly as fuel. Your focus should be on clean eating in moderation: lots of proteins, vegetables and fruits and only low-to-moderate carbs.

Junk food and soda consumed at sea level will stay on your waist for you to carry up to the summit, and these poor food choices can negatively impact your body's ability to summit successfully. At high elevations, your body processes carbohydrates more easily than proteins and fats; you should modify your mountain consumption accordingly. Admittedly, after a multi-day trek where I've burned thousands and thousands of calories, back in civilization a good burger or pizza really hits the spot!

When I first started trekking, I opted for MRE's (Meal-Ready-to-Eat/military rations) as they are pre-cooked, very filling, taste good, and contain everything you need for a complete meal, including spoon, condiments, beverage mix, snack, etc.

Sold at military surplus stores and some outdoor adventure stores, they are heavy, usually weighing between 1-2 pounds each, as they are not dehydrated, and have lots of rugged packaging to allow them to last in storage between three and 10 years.

You can shave a ton of weight by removing nearly all of the packaging and non-essentials down to just the wrapped main course. *Expert MRE tip: We've been programmed for years to hold a package vertically and just tear the top off where the pre-cut mark is on the package, however I learned from a trekking partner, who spent time in the Army, to turn the MRE horizontally and tear a U-shape from the top middle section. This way the spoon will reach every corner of the food pouch without getting food contents all over your hands!*

I've since shifted to freeze-dried meals for multi-day treks. This means you'll need to carry a camp stove, fuel, cup to boil water, etc.; however, the weight of a freeze-dried main course is around four ounces, and in most cases these meals taste a lot better than MRE's. There are usually more culinary options available, as well.

There may be times where you need to get a meal in you fast, and you are unable to boil water in a timely fashion (or because your trekking partner's stove caught on fire and was destroyed due to the wrong fuel being used!). I have found that MRE's do taste good cold and are much better than a freeze-dried meal with cold water added. *(Note that the latter does work in an emergency!)*

Complementing MRE's or freeze-dried food with energy bars, trail mix, etc. is a solid strategy to eat well in the mountains, as it allows you to continue to fuel your body throughout the day as you put in the work at altitude.

Ultimately, this mix of muscular strength, fatigue-fighting strength, an iron constitution, battling food- and water- borne bacteria, hygiene, inoculations, and nutrition will keep you healthy and fit in the mountains.

STRENGTH #2: CARDIOVASCULAR STRENGTH

....

"If you want to train for big mountain endeavors, spend time in big mountains."
– Jimmy Chin

Closely tied to Physical Strength is Cardiovascular Strength. Having great cardiovascular strength is obviously different than being physically strong. Picture the physique and training of a triathlete versus that of a bodybuilder. A bodybuilder typically lifts extremely heavy weights with lower repetitions to increase muscle mass, becoming ripped and gaining extreme strength. A triathlete lifts lighter weights with higher repetitions to increase endurance, complemented by functional fitness activities such as running, swimming and biking to increase their rate of breathing and get the heart pumping, while maintaining flexibility. This approach of building good cardiovascular strength is known to have many benefits, including lower blood pressure, a decreased risk for heart disease, etc. Trekking requires this same strategy for optimal performance.

For the trekker, cardio exercises are necessary to build up your lung capacity, increase the oxygen intake to your heart, and improve your stamina and endurance for the long haul in the mountains. While it takes physically strong legs to trek with that 50-pound pack, you also need top-notch cardiovascular fitness to do it mile after mile, day after day at elevation.

To build cardiovascular strength for the mountains, I'd recommend a regime of:

- **Stairmaster** to increase heart rate while using a similar motion as you would ascending a mountain pass. Add your backpack while performing this exercise to push yourself even harder.

- **Trail running** – On a foul weather day, you may prefer hitting the treadmill or the elliptical machine to increase cardio. Add the backpack here too.
- **Biking** – I prefer mountain biking off-road as typically the terrain is more varied, and you avoid dodging cars and pedestrians.
- **Weight training** using low weights and high reps.
- **Swimming** is a low impact way to increase cardiovascular capacity.
- **Martial Arts** – I enjoy Brazilian Jiu Jitsu as a way to increase cardio and endurance.

Before I started hiking years ago, I never really felt that my cardio was any good. But after putting in the miles on the trail, accomplishing treks with 100+ miles of hiking, or summiting 4 peaks in 48 hours in the Sierra Nevada high country, or driving from San Jose to Yosemite and hiking 19 miles to Half Dome and back then returning to San Jose that same day, I discovered I had a different type of endurance from all this training: one optimized for the mountains.

> *"The harder I train, the luckier I get."*
> *– Renzo Gracie*

Sprinting — Cardiovascular strength is absolutely critical in areas where you need to sprint to stay safe, as we discovered while winter camping in the Lake Tahoe area of Northern California. We set up base camp, strapped the snowshoes back on, and headed to an ascent of one of the nearby peaks. Snow began falling heavily. After reaching the summit, we descended rapidly to get back to the camp and hunker down. We were a mile or so from our camp when we saw a patch of bare mountain that clearly looked like a former avalanche path, was now covered in rapidly accumulating snow. Knowing that it looked sketchy, we spread ourselves out, and moved through this section one at a time. It was necessary to move briskly, yet carefully, through this avalanche-prone area, and having cardiovascular strength enabled us to traverse it with safety and speed. Cardiovascular fitness also plays an important role in moving efficiently yet cautiously through hazardous rock fall-prone terrain sections as well.

Sense of Urgency — In the next chapter on Altitudinal Strength, I'll advise not to race up a mountain in an effort to mitigate potential altitude sickness. However, here's something every trekker should keep in mind: *There needs to be a certain sense of urgency in the mountains.*

Moving briskly to get to the next camp before darkness falls or the big storm hits is imperative. So, it's necessary to achieve a balance between cardio and altitudinal strength. Experience and prudence will help dictate when you need to move quickly (using cardiovascular strength), and when you should proceed slowly up the mountain as not to accelerate the onslaught of altitude sickness.

Stretching — Warming up before each day's trek is essential. Cold muscles restrict flexibility and tear more easily. Stretching is an excellent way to warm up muscles, enhance flexibility, and avoid injury. Flexibility is imperative if you're navigating up or down terrain that is rocky, vertical, or requires scrambling. Begin each stretch slowly and gently and avoid bouncing to prevent inadvertent tearing. With each pull, hold for 10–20 seconds, and then slowly release. Do this several times and try to stretch a little bit more each time to increase the range of motion and flexibility. Be sure to breathe in through the nose and out through the mouth slowly as you stretch - never hold your breath. I would recommend the following stretches to ensure you're warmed up before you hit the trail:

- **Hurdle stretch** stretches the hamstring. I like adding **ankle rotations** to this stretch to get the ankles warmed up.
- **Butterfly stretch** stretches the inner thighs, groin, and hips.
- **Quad pulls** while standing upright stretch the quadricep muscles.
- **Calf stretch** — the motion of pulling your toes toward your body stretches your calf muscles. Also effective are lunging calf stretches, heel drop stretches, or having the ball of your foot against a tree or rock and gently leaning forward to stretch the calf.
- **Trunk twists** loosen up the lower back and core.
- **Arm rotations** to loosen up the shoulders.

I have always found cardio workouts to be the most challenging. However, paying your dues by pushing yourself in a cardiovascular way and relishing being drenched from the workout with your lungs "on fire", will absolutely increase your chance of success during the long miles on the trek. Investing in this fashion, for a few months in advance of the hike, will certainly pay dividends in the mountains.

"Endurance is one of the most difficult disciplines, but it is to the one who endures that the final victory comes."
— Gautama Buddha

STRENGTH #3: ALTITUDINAL STRENGTH

*"When you're climbing at high altitudes
life can get pretty miserable."*
— Sir Edmund Hillary

I call the ability of your body to successfully acclimatize at altitude, "Altitudinal Strength." Being physically strong with great cardio is key to successful summiting, as I've already discussed, but it's not enough.

One of my trekking partners on Mount Kilimanjaro was an accomplished marathon runner who biked more than 30 miles a day. Yet despite his excellent conditioning, he incurred cerebral edema on the roof of Africa.

Being mentally and physically strong was also not enough for another trekking partner. He managed to survive many hours in the open waters of the south Pacific when his boat flipped over during a massive storm that hit in the middle of the night. Yet he was hit by pulmonary edema the night before reaching Mount Everest Base Camp.

I tell you these cautionary tales not to scare you, but to convince you that you ignore the debilitating effects of high altitude at your own peril. Getting to the top of a big mountain over 8,000 feet (the point where altitude sickness may kick in) requires a clear strategy for the acclimatization process, and an intense awareness of the symptoms of Acute Mountain Sickness (AMS), High Altitude Pulmonary Edema (HAPE: fluid in the lungs) and High Altitude Cerebral Edema (HACE: fluid between the brain and skull). A laser-like focus on the progress of symptoms and an understanding of how to mitigate and when to seek medical help is absolutely essential and may mean the difference between life and death.

Expose Yourself to Higher Elevations in preparation for the big climb. While your genetic makeup largely determines how you will fare at acclimatizing, gradually working your way up to higher mountains over time is a solid strategy for understanding how your body will react at altitude, versus trying to summit Mount Kilimanjaro at over 19,000 feet your first time trekking straight from sea-level. In the months preceding the ascent of a big mountain, spend time at elevation as much as you can. It would be worth the investment to spend several days in the high country of California (Sierra Nevada Mountains) or Colorado (Rocky Mountains), where the mountain towns are nearly a mile high and the mountains themselves reach upwards of 14,000 feet.

Look/Listen/Feel for Symptoms of Hypoxia – If you or your climbing partners experience the symptoms of hypoxia (altitude sickness), take action immediately. Symptoms include:

- headache,
- upset stomach/nausea and/or loss of appetite,
- swelling of the hands and feet,
- coughing,
- tingling extremities,
- dizziness,
- light-headedness,
- difficulty breathing/trouble catching breath,
- blue lips (cyanosis),

- sloshing of fluid in lungs,
- coughing up fluid,
- vomiting,
- confusion,
- inability to focus,
- trouble standing up or walking in a straight line.

Don't Climb Higher – Descend Immediately! – If altitude sickness symptoms do not improve, or if they get worse, you need to descend immediately. The general guideline is to descend at least 1,000 feet for mild symptoms, and to descend 3,000 - 4,000 feet or completely off the mountain for moderate-to-severe symptoms. This truly is the best way to reduce the harmful impact of altitude sickness on your body.

Never Trek Alone and Never Leave Anybody Alone with symptoms of altitude sickness. If altitude sickness comes on rapidly and you or your trekking partner gets dizzy, one wrong step on a sketchy slope could easily be life-threatening. Cerebral and pulmonary edema on their own are deadly, but coupling this with impaired judgement, dizziness, trouble standing up, etc., when there's dangerous terrain around you is a recipe for disaster.

Increase Altitude Gradually – A general rule is to limit your ascent to 1,000 feet or less in a day to avoid altitude sickness. Design your trek accordingly. When we climbed Mt. Kilimanjaro, we purposefully chose the longest route that the guide company offered to maximize our chances for acclimatization and summit success. We even selected which company to go with based on the one who offered the longest trek. This is a tough trade-off, especially for new trekkers; it means keeping a more measured pace up the mountain, but also means more days and therefore more $$$, more time away from family, and more days away from work. It's a difficult sacrifice, but experience has shown that it's worth the investment.

Also, consider incorporating "rest days" every 3,000 vertical feet. This will accelerate acclimatization and also allow the legs, shoulders, core, and feet to take a much-needed break to recover. I recommend that you make it an "active rest day," incorporating easy day hikes to keep the body moving and acclimatizing (while taking in some great scenery). The last thing you want is to stiffen up from lying in your tent all day.

Climb High/Sleep Low — Typically, altitude sickness symptoms get worse at night due to problems acclimatizing to the new altitude reached during the day. "Climb high/sleep low" is another formula for success in the mountains. It involves pushing yourself to get to a higher altitude during the day, and then descending in the afternoon to sleep at a lower elevation at night. This will enable the body to adjust to the increase in altitude and get much-needed sleep, which is more difficult to achieve with the thin air.

Deep Breathing — It's important to maximize the oxygen you're pulling out of the air. To do this, focus on slowing down your breathing. Inhale deeply through the nose and exhale out the mouth. You'll know when you're breathing deeply when you see your chest rise and your abdomen expand with each inhale. Also, try to synchronize the rhythm of your breaths with the rhythm of your steps. Some recommend pressure breathing with pursed lips, but I found that too hard to internalize. The approach I've outlined above is similar to the breathing I've used for years in martial arts and strength training, so it feels more natural to me.

Consume Adequate Liquids — Staying well-hydrated is critical on the mountain. Even when it's cold or overcast, your body is still processing water. Invest in a hydration bladder which will allow you to sip water at approximately the same rate as your body is processing it.

If your urine is dark yellow, you are dehydrated. If you feel parched or have "cotton mouth," you are dehydrated.

You should be consuming 4+ quarts of water per day at altitude but be aware that not all liquids are created equal. Your best bets are water (purified), sports drinks with added electrolytes (such as Gatorade), soups, and low-caffeine hot teas (for example, green tea). Avoid alcohol and caffeine-heavy drinks, which are diuretics that will further dehydrate you. Drinking caffeinated beverages late in the day could disrupt an already challenging sleep cycle.

Avoid Excessively Strenuous Exertion from carrying heavy loads up the mountain and putting your body in overdrive while you're trying to acclimatize. Incorporate rest and recovery days and consider hiring porters to help.

Dress Strategically – It's important to manage perspiration to avoid overheating or rapid cooling. The latter can be an issue at altitude, because blood vessels may constrict when the body cools quickly, which may limit optimal oxygen transport to your organs. See the chapter on gear preparation for further explanation of dressing strategically.

Consider Preventive Prescription Medicines like Acetazolamide (Diamox) and gingko biloba, or even Dexamethasone for emergencies. I've never used any of these medications, but with a doctor's advice and prescription and when used correctly, these have shown to lessen the effects of altitude on climbers. Note that you will need to start any course of medication prior to arriving at altitude, so plan in advance.

Even though you'll probably be craving a solid night's sleep, sleeping pills are not recommended as they suppress breathing and can depress your blood oxygen levels. This is not a good thing, especially at high elevations. Please speak with your primary care physician about how these and other medications might affect you at altitude.

As I was writing this chapter, there were visceral incidents during my Everest Base Camp trek and Kilimanjaro trek that immediately popped into my mind. These notes below are from my journal during those treks and highlight the impact that altitude might have on a trekker at altitude:

A) **Altitude is not for Everybody** – *The lodge at Pheriche was immaculate and jam-packed with tourists, many of whom seemed to be completely out of their leagues – really suffering from the physical effort, and more profoundly, the altitude. All throughout the day and night we would hear rescue helicopters taking tourists with altitude sickness back down the mountain.*

B) **Pulmonary Edema** - *On the Everest Base Camp trek, I noticed my climbing partner had a lingering cough the past couple of days. As we're about to hit the sack for the night, Chris rolls over and says, "Hey can you hear that?" He rolls over again and indeed I can – despite being on the other side of the room, what I'm hearing is fluid sloshing around in his lungs due to high altitude pulmonary edema. We had the conversation that the best thing for him to do was descend the mountain before it got worse. He pushed back and would not have it – he was going to continue the climb and fight through it (note: this is not advised!). He is, amongst other things, a sailor who in one of his many Sydney-to-Hobart Tasmania yacht races was stuck in a massive storm which flipped his team's boat in the middle of the night. After hours and hours in the heart of a violent storm, which* was tossing the seas, the crew, and their boat in the black of the night, they managed to be rescued. Talk about mental strength! So, his rationale was that a little pulmonary edema was not going to get in his way. We agreed to monitor it closely and reassess accordingly. I listened carefully throughout the night and would do so while we remained at altitude the next 24 hours.

C) **Cerebral Edema** - *Conversation at the summit was a joke as none of us were able to get a clear sentence out due to the lack of sleep. A few minutes later my climbing partner approached. His face was white as a ghost and his eyes were failing to focus. He looked like he had 15 beers and was stumbling everywhere. I immediately said, "You need to descend now." This was cerebral edema in black and white. The guide turned to my climbing partner and asked, "What do you think?" He responded, "One more try". This section between Stella Point (18,871 feet) and Uhuru Summit (19,341 feet) was extremely icy and slick due to the wet weather the prior several days and it was freezing at these high elevations. My climbing partner slid all over the place and could barely stay vertical while just trying to take those couple steps – he was a danger to himself and others (flailing trekking poles are weapons!) We quickly took a few photos and he proceeded to descend down the mountain with the guide. With cerebral edema, rapid descent is the only real solution.*

D) **Successful Acclimatization** – *I reflected on what a great night's sleep I had that night at Pheriche (13,730 feet) after descending from Everest Base Camp and Kala Patthar. I finally feel like I had fully acclimatized at that stage. In fact, the one thing that I recalled is that I felt stronger with each day that passed. Every day built upon the prior days' journey, a slow, methodical acclimatization with many days pushing higher and higher on the mountain, and with several opportunities to climb high and sleep low. At this stage I have spent 4 days trekking over 17,000 feet, and 3 of the 4 hitting over 18,000 feet (Chukhung Ri - 18,200 feet, Kongma-La Pass – 18,100 feet, Everest Base Camp – 17,600 feet, and Kala Patthar – 18,500 feet).*

Altitudinal Strength will make or break your high-altitude adventure. Again, not to scare you, but this is one that has the potential for being life or death if symptom-recognition and immediate mitigation is ignored. Listen to your body and be open and honest with your guide and trekking party about how you are feeling and acclimatizing. It's a good idea to implement the buddy system in your trekking group. Each pair of buddies will keep a careful eye on each other and check in frequently to see how well their buddy is acclimatizing. The lead guide should also be in tune to the trekking party's wellbeing. If you have to turn around, that's okay; I'm sure there are plenty of absolutely beautiful vistas at a slightly lower altitude, that will still be a magnitude greater than sitting at work or in traffic back in civilization!

"When I went to Everest, I underestimated things. I just didn't know what altitude could do. Or the cold – I especially didn't appreciate the cold. It can be just debilitating, and things can happen so quickly."
– Jon Krakauer

Disclaimer: This is not intended to be a medical journal about altitude sickness. The steps highlighted have worked for me, but as everyone reacts differently at altitude, it is strongly advised that the reader do their own research and consult their physician before partaking in high altitude activities.

The Seven Strengths of Summiting | **Mark Santino**

STRENGTH #4: MENTAL, EMOTIONAL AND SPIRITUAL STRENGTH

....

*"Strength does not come from physical capacity.
It comes from an indomitable will."*
— Mahatma Gandhi

Even if you've done all the physical preparation and are feeling strong at altitude, it's quite possible you still may not reach your objectives. You can't control what the mountain will throw at you, and how you respond to adverse situations, from a mental and emotional perspective, will ultimately determine your success.

Mental Strength boils down to:

- Mental toughness and mental endurance – having the ability to persevere in stressful situations and to push forward despite obstacles.
- Being calm and patient under pressure; having the inner fortitude to weather the storm.
- The wisdom to expect the unexpected.
- Being comfortable with being uncomfortable.
- Having a positive and optimistic outlook.

A significant part of the preparation process is to consider every possible scenario that might transpire. Take the time to think through what could happen on the mountain, and how you would handle each potential situation. And remember: You also need a backup plan (or two). The worst time to figure out a solution to a problem is when you're at altitude and dealing with multiple complex issues at once. Be smart; plan ahead.

That being said, you can't plan for everything. Despite climbing Mount Kilimanjaro during the dry season, heavy rains fell on the mountain for days. This hadn't happened in decades, and while we were prepared with waterproof gear, our porters were not outfitted to handle this freak weather, and all the gear, including ours, was completely soaked. Sadly, two porters from another trekking party, two days ahead of us on the mountain, died from exposure. Processing death in the mountains and having serious discussions about turning around and canceling the summit attempt weigh heavily when you're in rarefied air in a different continent halfway around the world. Fortunately, I carried exclusively synthetic gear, so even though it was wet, my sleeping bag kept me warm. All night long I wore wet clothes, swapping them out as they dried from my body heat, so I'd have dry gear for the next day. I persisted in this task throughout the exhaustion I felt, because I was determined to overcome this obstacle, control what I was able to control, and get back on track.

While trekking the Inca Trail to Machu Picchu, one of our party members lost his passport on the flight out of the US, and was stuck in the airport in Lima, Peru for several days. We were already in Cusco, but we worked remotely with the local Embassy to negotiate with the Peruvian government and airport security to allow him to stay at airport hotel instead of sleeping on the floor of the airport while they worked on reissuing his passport. This process took several days and challenged all of us to keep our cool and be patient. In a delicate situation like this, raging emotions and raised voices will get you nowhere.

On another trek, while winter camping in the Sierra Nevada Mountains in Northern California, a snowstorm hit us so hard that the weight of the snow collapsed our only tent. The moral of the story is that you must be prepared for anything and expect the unexpected.

Culture Shock – One thing is certain: You will experience some form of culture shock. It's impossible to prepare completely for the unfamiliar sights, smells, sounds, customs, and general chaos in some of these locations. For example, before even reaching the mountains, you may find yourself in Kathmandu dodging rabid dogs on the streets, walking past blazing funeral pyres, be stranded without transportation because of a day-long incendiary protest against the government, and seeing 4-inch-long leeches climbing up your shower wall. Also, in today's age of near-addiction to electronics and connectivity, having no Wi-Fi, cell reception, or fresh batteries can give you withdrawal!

Avoid Being Overwhelmed – In the mountains, you may be physically spent, experiencing pain and exhaustion, or overwhelmed by a significant challenge. Taking each obstacle one at a time is key. Breaking down a big goal into smaller, manageable milestones are not only less daunting; it also builds confidence as you successfully tackle each sub-goal. Focus on small successes: set your sights on just getting to that rock in the distance, and as you near this target, pick the next rock or tree and focus on that as your next goal. If you just stare at the summit thinking it's too far/too high/too painful/too exhausting, you may not make it. Also, you often see what looks like the summit, only to realize once you get closer that it's a false summit— that can cause you to think about turning back around. It's important to remember that the true summit is getting home – *all* the way home, not just back to the tent. Reaching the summit is just the first half of the journey, so you need to plan accordingly (in terms of physical and mental energy, water, food, daylight, etc.) to live to fight and trek another day.

The night before "summit day" on our Everest Base Camp trek, my trekking partner developed pulmonary edema due to the altitude. Here's a guy who's tough as nails – he frequently competed in multi-day/night yacht-races up the Australian coast. On one memorable occasion, when a severe storm flipped his boat over in the middle of the night, he stayed calm and followed the agreed-upon emergency protocols. Surviving an overturned boat in rough, potentially shark-infested ocean waters in complete darkness gave him the mental stamina to push aside any minor annoyances and roadblocks we faced on our trek and allowed him to maintain the focus he needed to reach our goal.

Balancing Prudence with Perseverance – On Mount Whitney (my first major trek and summit over 14,000 feet), we faced a challenging mix of altitude and a massive storm. The only thing protecting us from the elements was a cheap camping tent tethered to as many rocks as we could find. At any moment it could have been shredded due to the heavy winds, but miraculously, it weathered the onslaught. The trekkers we met just 24 hours earlier weren't so lucky – the wind literally blew their tent off the mountain.

At 12,000 feet, we set the alarm for an early start while it was still dark. When we began ascending, we encountered three trekkers who had bivouacked in their emergency blankets, shivering profoundly and counting the minutes until the sun peeked over the ridge and begin to warm them. We discovered that our water source had begun to freeze overnight. The water turned to ice as it entered the bottles. When some of it spilled on me, the risk of getting hypothermia because of my wet clothes freaked me out, but the water instantly froze on my jacket and pants, and I was able to literally brush it off. We were naive; instead of being scared by these warning signs, they invigorated us to push ahead and explore the personal unknown.

> *"If you think you can do a thing or think you can't do a thing, you're right."*
> *– Henry Ford*

Emotional Strength – Emotions can run high in the mountains. You're dealing with some challenging lows – altitude, culture shock, complete exhaustion, bitter cold and wind, being cramped in a tent with a snoring trekking partner, etc. – and the most exhilarating highs: magnificent sunsets, views for miles, wildlife you just read about in books, wonderfully warm locals, crisp clean mountain air, incredible sense of accomplishment of reaching a difficult section of the trail, etc. These feelings aren't binary; you can experience a number of ups and downs in a single day, and even in a single hour. To cope, it all starts with self-awareness. Are you overreacting? Is the flood of emotions overwhelming? Label the negative feelings and ask if the situation is something you can control. If you can't control it, try to put your reaction to it out of your mind.

Of course, your team may be experiencing similar emotions. It's important to listen and be aware of non-verbal cues, such as a normally talkative buddy who hasn't said a word in hours. Be empathetic to what they might be going through – try to talk it out with one of your trekking buddies to work through it together. Also, it may help to try to capture your emotions on paper; things may make more sense when you see them written down in black and white. I also find that gratitude is critical to regulating your mood: Be grateful for the opportunity to be in the mountains; for sharing the experience with good friends; for experiencing a new culture and learning more about the world (and yourself); be grateful you're not stuck in traffic, heading to work while breathing in pollution from the tractor trailer that's going to make you late for that important meeting!

> **"Oh, these vast, calm, measureless mountain days, days in whose light everything seems equally divine, opening a thousand windows to show us God."**
> *– John Muir*

Spiritual Strength – Not everyone believes in a higher being, and the definition of spiritual strength varies widely. When I'm in the wilderness, I feel extraordinarily grateful and blessed to have the opportunity to see such amazing landscapes, mountains, lakes, cultures, and people, and the expression "God's country" instantly comes to mind. It's hard to deny the absolute beauty of these places, and I am always in awe of the magnificence that abounds in nature. In every continent I've trekked, the local people revere the mountains; many believe the mountains are sacred and are the home to their God(s). It's therefore important to be respectful of the mountains (for example, abstaining from alcohol) and the local religious beliefs. My thoughts and prayers throughout the trek involve the safety of our team and the locals who are helping us, and my family at home. And, I thank God for the opportunity to experience the world's wonders.

Example of Spiritual Strength in the Himalayas – *Excerpt from Appendix B:* *I woke to the sounds of long horns blowing. Given that Tengboche is a Tibetan Monastery village, we knew it must be important. I then heard a knock on the door. It was Raj our guide, who said a High Lama was arriving and there would be a ceremony in the temple. I quickly grabbed my camera and some cash for a donation. There were three Tibetan Monks in the beautiful monastery when we arrived. We stuck around and after all the tourists thinned out, Raj arranged for the highest Monk/Lama to perform a brief ceremonial blessing and to place a prayer scarf, known as a Khata, around my neck as a blessing to protect us during our journey in the mountains. It was very special to receive the blessing and Khata.*

Example of Spiritual Strength in Africa – *Excerpt from Appendix C:* *Before embarking on the Kilimanjaro trek, Emmy, the guide company's local director, was very emotional as she told us that* her people, the Chagga, see the mountain as holy and she said she prayed for us to have a safe and successful trek.

Giving back — In Nepal, we visited Khumjung and saw the school that Sir Edmund Hillary built. A few years prior to our trek, a group of volunteers helped to establish internet connectivity on Base Camp, to enable critical communications, including weather conditions and safety on the mountain.

I realized that we missed an opportunity to give something back to the community we would be gaining so much from. In Tanzania, we "righted that wrong" by putting together a charitable campaign to benefit the Amani Centre for Street Children in Arusha. This charity is doing incredible work at the foot of Mount Kilimanjaro. It really is fulfilling to trek for a greater purpose and help the local community, turning the trip from an essentially selfish adventure travel event into something much bigger. A dollar goes a long way in some of these communities, so the impact of a successful campaign can really be profound.

> **"Physical strength can never permanently withstand the impact of spiritual force."**
> **– Franklin D. Roosevelt**

Global Citizen — The more global travel and adventure I've experienced, the more of a global citizen I feel I have become, enhancing personal cultural awareness with every trip. Every interaction is a way to let the locals, and even the other tourists that we meet, know that we are in fact "typical Americans" and what they hear on the news or how we're stereotyped in the media or in movies is not necessarily reality. I've noticed that despite our differences, there is a global sameness: The world is made up of genuinely good people who are focused on their families and friends, their higher mission or higher being, looking for a reason to smile and connect in their own way. In general, people live a more non-material/simple lifestyle and find that people make them happy, and not things. (Americans have a lot to learn here!)

"Keep close to Nature's heart... and break clear away once in a while and climb a mountain or spend a week in the woods. Wash your spirit clean."
– John Muir

STRENGTH #5: TEAM STRENGTH

....

"There is something about building up a comradeship – that I still believe is the greatest of all feats – and sharing in the dangers with your company of peers. It's the intense effort, the giving of everything you've got. It's really a very pleasant sensation."
– Sir Edmund Hillary

I firmly believe that trekking in the mountains (and adventure travel in general), is best enjoyed as a team sport. While it's incredibly rewarding to experience amazing mountains around the world, it's even more rewarding to share those experiences with like-minded adventurers. Aside from the fun to be had, teamwork and collaboration are a critical element in any successful expedition. Team communications, group problem-solving processes, decision-making dynamics, etc., will all influence how successful your adventure will be.

Things to consider:

- **Choosing your Trekking/Climbing Team**

How many trekkers? It's understandable that you may want to share your passion for the mountains with everyone you know. However, keep in mind that the larger the team, the trickier the logistics will be. In my experience, a team of 2-5 is optimal. If there are more than that, it may be best to split up into two smaller teams.

- **Team Like-mindedness**

A little discussion ahead of time will work wonders for team dynamics. The most effective teams are likely those whose members have common outdoor interests, destination preferences, fitness levels, budget considerations, and risk profiles. Since you'll be spending a lot of time with the people on your team and will depend on them to work together for a successful trek, it makes sense to carefully vet each potential member to make sure the fit is optimal.

- **Team Trekking Ability and Overall Experience**

Picture this: You're roped together, ascending Mount Shasta, nearing 14,000 feet. If one climber falls, the rest of team needs to self-arrest and hold the fallen climber. Your life could *literally* be in your teammates' hands. To balance out the pace and maximize safety for our rope team of four, the lead (most experienced) climber was in the first position, and the next strongest was last. If your trek includes one very experienced trekker and 8 completely inexperienced trekkers, for example, it's vital that you choose a destination suitable for those experience levels. When climbing at high altitude, the dangers are very real, and stacking your team with beginners is a recipe for disaster.

- **Pace of Climb/Trek**

Pacing is a delicate balance that involves (1) pushing the slower trekkers to keep moving in order to maximize remaining daylight hours and avoid less-than-ideal weather systems that might be racing in, and (2) reigning in the faster trekkers, so the group doesn't get split up unintentionally where the group makes a wrong turn or passes camp, etc.

- **Look Out for Each Other (Buddy System)**

As I previously mentioned, it's a good idea to use the buddy system on long high-altitude climbs. A buddy will notice if you're not drinking enough water or eating enough; experiencing altitude symptoms; having abnormally frequent bathroom breaks due to diarrhea; are struggling with the pace or showing signs of physical wear and tear (such as limping); or wearing the right gear (Are your glacier glasses on when in area of potential snow-blindness? Are your trekking poles out on sketchy terrain? Are your crampons on when crossing the snow and ice field?) Knowing that someone has your back on a difficult trek provides peace of mind and another layer of protection for everyone on the team.

"My work is all about adventure and teamwork in some of the most inhospitable jungles, mountains and deserts on the planet. If you aren't able to look after yourself and each other, then people die."
– Bear Grylls

Decision Making Process

Earlier, I briefly discussed the need for ensuring everyone on the trek has the same general mindset. I'd like to expand on that a bit more.

Before you arrive in the mountains, it's critical that you reach an agreement with your trekking partners on (a) decisions that must be made ahead of time and (b) how decisions will be made as issues crop up during the trek. For example:

- Will someone take on the role of Trek Leader/Lead Guide?
- Who decides? The Trek Leader? Pure democracy?
- What other roles and responsibilities will others take, both during preparation, and on the trip itself?
- What's your team communication process? If split up, will cell phones work, do you have a pair of Satellite phones, or will you have 2-way radios? Are there dedicated check points where the two teams will physically reconnect if communications go down?
- How will you split up team common gear? In many instances, it won't make sense to have every single trekker carry duplicate gear up the mountain. For example, if we bring a two-man tent, to split the weight, does one person carry the main body of the tent and the other carry the rain fly plus tent poles and stakes? If one member brings the stove, who will carry the fuel? If the group splits up, will the gear split up as well? Or do you want to make sure one half of the group at least has a stove, fuel, water purifier, tent, etc., so there is no exposure?

- What time will you start the trek each morning? Will you get up at the crack of dawn, or sleep in a little bit to recover your strength after a difficult day yesterday?
- How much distance will you aim to cover each day?
- When will the turnaround time be on Summit Day? What will you do if you're close to summit but it's already turnaround time?
- What will you do if bad weather is forecast? End the trip early? Change the campsite? Change the route?
- When will you choose another route if the planned route is not viable or downright dangerous (for example a chance of rain increasing the flash flood risk in a slot canyon traverse)?
- What are the deciding factors to send an impaired climber down the mountain? How will it be decided who escorts this impaired climber down the mountain?
- How do you balance the requests of the mountain "maximizer" (the mountain opportunist who's always trying to tack on additional side trails and scenic routes, wanting to take pictures during the most precarious sections of a route, wanting to hit a better route despite the increased risk, etc.)?

I've been trekking/climbing with a great friend for over 20 years, and here's how we handle it:

Typically, when we organize a trekking event, he and I are the most experienced, and both assume the "Co-Lead Guide" role. As Co-Lead Guides, we not only have responsibility for most of the logistical planning (including optimal travel arrival and departures, booking aspects of the trip – permits, campsites, guide companies, etc.– route planning, gear planning, food planning, and the like), but also have responsibility for making some of the decisions on behalf of the whole trekking team. This means determining routes that the entire group can handle, breaking the trip's mileage into daily chunks that work for each member (which usually stretches some of the team and slows down others), with the goal of sticking together as a group. We need alignment to ensure the best interests of the team (and their families) are considered, and then typically present these vetted options to the team for a final decision.

Family Strength – Another part of the team is the family back at home waiting for your return. If your significant other enjoys the mountains, you're in great shape! I've occasionally seen couples and families trekking together in the wilderness, but frankly, they're the exception. To avoid resentments on the home front, I recommend balancing buddy adventures with family adventures. Even if the family adventures aren't as extreme, there are plenty of global experiences and outdoor activities at all difficulty levels to last a lifetime.

I think frequently of my family while I'm in the mountains; absence really does make the heart grow fonder! I think of my wife and children as I make decisions during the trek always erring on the side of caution and knowing that I'm one day closer to seeing them motivates me to push through the challenges of the day.

> *"Alone we can do so little, together we can do so much."*
> *– Helen Keller*

The Seven Strengths of Summiting | **Mark Santino**

STRENGTH #6:
PREPARATION STRENGTH

....

*"Success depends upon previous preparation,
and without such preparation there is sure to be failure."*
– Confucius

There are major steps required to prepare for a trek. To ensure it goes smoothly, I advise spending a material amount of time, far in advance of your trek, to organize and prepare. The more you plan, the less room you leave for failure or negative surprises while you're on the mountain. These are the major steps, but be aware, there's a lot of follow-up required. This is especially true if you've committed to taking a lead role on your trekking team, in which case you'll want to make sure that your entire team is as well-prepared as you are.

Determine Adventure Destination

With the trekking team, start making your list of potential destinations immediately. There are so many incredible places to choose from, both domestically and internationally. Here in the U.S., we're blessed with an amazing National Park system. Internationally, you'll find an extraordinary number of awe-inspiring national parks and World Heritage sites to choose from. Take your time and research your options thoroughly. A quick Amazon search will turn up tons of books that catalogue the best places to explore around the world. The amount of information available on the internet can be a bit overwhelming, but it's worth taking the time to extensively research in advance.

When we were preparing for a day hike up the Knife Edge route on Mount Katahdin in Maine, I mistakenly read that there was a sketchy 50 foot section along the Knife Edge route, so mentally I was preparing for a slow and careful traverse of this relatively short but dangerous section. It turned out that this 50-foot section was actually a 1½ mile-long Knife Edge that was as narrow as four feet wide with 2000-foot drop offs on either side. This would have been brutal as it was, but just after we began the trek, and unbeknownst to us, the Park Rangers closed the trail due to high winds. In the middle of the massively dangerous ridge, the 35-45 mph winds kicked into full gear. We were literally hanging on for dear life. After hours and hours of carefully placed footholds, lots of praying, and much cursing, we managed to complete the section. *Detailed planning is essential.* That "short 50-foot section" could have been catastrophic for us.

In terms of choosing the adventure itself, it's best to start small and work your way up to bigger adventures/mountains. The experience you gain along the way will be critical in the preparation for the big ones, and ultimately enable a more enjoyable, safe and successful experience.

Acquire guidebooks and maps

I recommend getting guidebooks and maps as soon as you choose the destination. Amazon has every option you can imagine. I've found that some local guidebooks and maps are only available in the mountain shops or park headquarters at the destination, but I wouldn't wait to obtain these or assume you'll be able to find the map you need just as you're about to start the trek. Plan ahead and you might be able to supplement the guidebooks and maps you have when you arrive.

When choosing maps, consider the following: (a) getting an overview map of the area to give you the lay of the land, and help you choose where you specifically want to go, the routes you'll take, and in most cases, the local roads to get in and out; and (b) getting a detailed map (1:24,000 ratio is the best, if available) to help navigate the trails and terrain. Look for these to include *distances* from trail head to trail intersections, to sights along the way and the summits themselves. Be sure the map includes the *altitude* of these milestones, so you can match the contours of the maps, the identifying landmarks (like a river), and how long you've traveled to the altitude on your altimeter watch. Both types of maps will be essential for preparatory route planning, as well as when you are trekking on the trail. Even if you go with a guide company, do your homework so you know what your team is getting into and you can ask the right questions, and even while you're on a guided trek, always bring that map with you on the trails, for peace of mind and safety.

Determine timeframe

Finding a time when your entire team is available is important, of course, but you also need to make sure the timeframe you've chosen matches the optimal weather window for your destination. For example, if you want to climb Mount Fuji in April, but the mountain is only accessible in July and August this year, you'll be in for a big (and unpleasant) surprise when landing in Tokyo. And trust me – when it comes to the Himalayas, you really don't want to be trekking during monsoon season if you don't have to.

Select and book the guide company

I highly recommend hiring a guide company for most international adventures. It's great having locals who speak the language, understand how to get stuff done in the local culture (including navigating local geopolitical challenges), are trustworthy, etc. In some cases, whether to hire a guide company is up to the discretion of the trekking party, and in other cases it's mandatory. For example:

(a) Some treks absolutely require local guide support (for example, trekking in Bhutan);

(b) For others, it just makes a ton of sense due to the magnitude and extensive logistics of the destination (for example, Mount Kilimanjaro);

(c) On other treks, you may opt to get help from a guide company for in-country logistical planning, but then self-guide on the trek itself (as in the Haute Route in the Swiss/French Alps);

(d) And lastly, on some treks, a guide is really not needed at all (like hiking Mount Whitney).

You can find a lot of useful information, as well as guide company ratings and reviews, in guidebooks and on the internet. It's always best to have some idea of the experience you're looking for, so you don't get stuck with a standard cookie-cutter trek. As an example, in preparation for climbing Mount Kilimanjaro we:

a. Asked friends who had already climbed it which guide company they used, what route they took, how satisfied they were with the company, and if they would they recommend them.

b. Bought the Mount Kilimanjaro guidebook and checked out the routes and the guide companies they recommended.

c. Looked at the big name/first class American and British guide companies' websites, which spelled out day-to-day itineraries, mileage, altitude, routes, sights, etc. If they have exactly what you're looking for, at the price point you want, you might be able to stop here. However, the next step would typically be to:

d. Find a local (in-country) guide company that can offer the same high-quality service, at a more reasonable price point, where

(1) the profits benefit the local community (versus sending the profits overseas);

(2) the guide company is committed to "fair-trade" and paying their staff a good wage and benefits (note that these Fair Trade guide companies will cost a little more, but it's worth it as safety is a top priority, and the staff are usually happier and more interactive);

(3) the guide company gives back to the local community.

I've found that these local guide companies can easily accommodate requests like:

(a) adding an additional rest/acclimatization day;

(b) adding a side "trip" on the route;

(c) bolt-on sightseeing before and after the trek, etc.;

(d) also, if you have a dedicated guide for your group, with the guide company's agreement, you may be able to modify the trek on the fly as we did during our Mount Everest Base

Camp trek. Because we were feeling strong while we were in the middle of the guided trek, we spoke with the lead guide and we were able to adjust the route on the spot; we were able to traverse a high pass which enabled additional altitude exposure, avoided the crowds, and trimmed a day off the climb.

e. It's important to pick up the phone and talk to these companies. You can get a good read on the company based on how the call goes, how quickly they respond to your phone calls and emails, how thoroughly they answer your questions (or whether they tend to dodge questions), how organized and professional they sound, if they can share relevant statistics, such as what percentage of trekkers reach the summit, etc.

f. Lock in the guide company. Once you and the team decide which company to proceed with, I recommend booking right away, as popular companies with popular destinations at popular time windows will fill up quickly, months in advance. Ensure the specific trek route is specified, the airport pickups/drop-offs arranged, side excursions determined, dietary requirements confirmed, etc. Gain agreement on the communication channel and frequency with your contact at the guide company as well. Make sure to get a detailed day-to-day itinerary, including extensive details on altitude and distances throughout the trek, as well as the required gear list. Usually a deposit or full pre-payment will be required.

"Give me six hours to cut down a tree, and I will spend the first four sharpening the axe."
– Abraham Lincoln

Lock in flights, transportation, lodging

Do this immediately, as every other trekker and tourist will be trying to get optimal flights and lodging during this peak trekking window. You don't want to pay for the guide company, only to discover there's not a reasonably-priced seat available on the plane you need to get there, or that the plane arrives after the trek begins, etc. Consider tacking on a buffer day or two in both the front and the back of the trip to account for potential delays reaching the destination, or delays on the trail. You can use these days for local sightseeing, allowing your body to adjust to the time zone, altitude, local water/food (while there's a modern/clean bathroom nearby!) and day hikes to acclimatize.

Know where you're going

As part of your preparation, read about the region's geopolitical conditions, crime rates, tensions, demonstrations against the government, local insurgents, financial stability, whether labor strikes might impact your local transportation, areas to avoid, and most importantly, the contact info for the local embassies/consulates at the destination. The embassy information was priceless when one of our trekking partners lost their passport en route to Peru for our Inca Trail trek and got stuck in immigration security.

Key Contacts:
- General Information for Each Country:
    - https://www.state.gov/misc/list/index.htm
- Additional Current Travel Advisory/Alert for each country:
    - https://travel.state.gov/content/travel/en/traveladvisories/traveladvisories.html
- You can also register with the State Department so you can get alerts on your mobile device, and easily keep them informed of your whereabouts:
    - https://step.state.gov/

Get passports and visas

Some countries require only a passport (which must be valid for at least 6 months post-arrival in most cases), but some additionally require tourist visas. You can find this information on the U.S. State Department's travel country pages. The visa process can take several months, so start this process early. You won't be able to enter the country without the proper documentation.

Preparations for Staying Healthy

It's important to also be aware of what, if any, inoculations are recommended for the destination region. Some inoculations, like rabies, require multiple shots, several weeks in advance of the departure. The U.S. Center for Disease Control's (CDC) website is excellent to help guide you in this matter:
- https://wwwnc.cdc.gov/travel

Financial and currency preparation

Get your financial ducks in a row, too. Consider:

- Local currency preparation: While you may get by paying with U.S. dollars, credit cards or travelers checks while in-country, I always try to order some local currency several weeks before departure. If you're hoping to use the ATM or currency exchange at the airport and it's not functioning or it's closed when you arrive, it's nice to have some local currency to buy bottled water or pay for the taxi ride to the hotel. You may also need to pay the remaining portion of fees owed to the guide company when you arrive. Commonly, this can be paid with local currency, U.S. dollars, credit card, or travelers' checks. There are plenty of smart phone apps for converting currency; I typically use OANDA's currency converter when planning:
    - https://www.oanda.com/currency/converter/

- Financial preparation: If you'll be out of the U.S. for a while, ensure you have some extra cash in your checking account in case you need hit the ATM more than you expected, or if you have problem with your credit card. Also, any sort of automation on paycheck deposits and advance bill-pay will keep your head focused on the mountains, instead of trying to sort out finances at 14,000 feet in a different country.

- Credit card preparation: Notify your credit card company of the countries you'll be visiting so the fraud department doesn't inadvertently lock your card when you're paying the guide company for a side trip excursion, or have to get new boots before the trek starts because one of your suitcases was lost en route. While you're at it, find out how much they charge for foreign transaction fees or cash advances.

- Travel insurance is good to have in case of travel interruptions, injuries, or cancellations. It doesn't cost much, but the peace of mind it provides is priceless.

Power/Electricity Converters/Adaptors

110 (U.S.) versus 220 (International) volt differences can fry your devices. The plugs themselves are different in most countries. Get the required adapters and/or power converters in advance to save yourself the hassle of trying to track them down in the airport or around the city when you arrive in-country.

Communications

Before you go, notify your mobile cellular provider of your international travel, and ask if they have an affordable roaming plan you can join. An alternative is to pick up a pre-paid SIM card when you enter the destination country, which will allow you to make calls at a fraction of the cost. (*Please note that you should confirm in advance with your cellular provider that your phone can accept a foreign SIM card.*) If your trekking location is extremely remote, you may want to invest in a satellite phone for communications as the mobile networks may be unreliable or non-existent.

Before you go

Lastly, before you depart, provide family and/or emergency contacts with a copy of your exact itinerary, maps, routes, expected check-in/communication points, copy of key documents (passport, visa, ID, credit cards), embassy details, etc.

And, while you and your guide company have surely done a ton of planning and preparation, always remember to "trust but verify": double check you've got the critical gear, double check flight details, double check local transportation pickups, double check you've got your passport, etc.

"Before anything else, preparation is the key to success."
– Alexander Graham Bell

STRENGTH #7:
GEAR STRENGTH

....

"It's not about what the equipment does, it's about what you can do through that equipment. That's where the soul is."
– Richie Hawtin

Ah, gear! It protects you from the elements and enables you to stay comfortable – and ultimately survive – in the outdoors. *(And, living in northeastern United States, I've found I've been able to test gear just walking to the mailbox during the winter!)*

If your excursion preparation is inadequate, you may end up with the wrong gear for the trip/environment you're embarking upon. At worst, that could put you in danger in the high country, and at best cause you to be miserable if (a) you don't have the piece of gear you need, (b) your gear falls short from a functional perspective, or (c) it fails on you from a durability perspective.

Weather and Environment Conditions

Expected conditions will drive your gear preparation as well as your mental expectations. Questions to ask yourself ahead of time include:
- What **altitude** will you be at throughout the trek?
- What are the average **temperature** ranges?
- What type of **weather** can you expect? Will it be rainy season? Could you experience three seasons in a single day (sun, rain, snow, etc.)? In some mountain ranges this phenomenon is common.
- Will you be traversing an environment that will require **specialized gear**? For example:
    - In the desert, you might need a snake bite kit, sun protection, extra water, and tweezers to remove cactus spines.

- In a water/canyoneering environment, you'll need boots designed for traversing in water, a special wood hiking pole for balance and navigating submerged rocks (your aluminum or carbon trekking poles may bend if caught in a mix of rocks, mud, and flowing water), and dry bags to keep your gear from getting wet.
- In areas that experience flash floods, you'll need to plan for alternate routes.
- If there's heavy snow and ice, you'll need an ice axe, crampons, mountaineering boots, ropes, avalanche beacons, etc.
- Vertical terrain demands a climbing harness, helmet, ropes, climbing hardware, chalk bag, and climbing shoes.
- Bear country requires bear canisters, a bear bell, ropes for hanging your food and all your scented items such as toothpaste, deodorant, etc.
- For trails that don't have toilet facilities, the implements to bury your waste, or carry it out.

Gear Drivers

The weather will drive a number of your gear decisions, such as the tent/shelter requirement (i.e. Will you need a four-season tent to handle frigid snow and wind? Or a three-season tent with great ventilation and a rain fly? Or can you get by with just a bivy sack?) and outer layer choice (i.e. will you need a waterproof and breathable rain jacket, rain pants, and waterproof hat?) Most other gear questions can be answered based on the temperature and altitude of your trek.

Weather

For advice on what to expect, turn to guidebooks, your guide company, local park rangers, and your favorite weather app. However, you'll see that it is very hard to find a proper weather report for the specific peak you intend to summit — but don't fear, you should be able to find the weather for the nearest Ranger Station. Performing some basic temperature calculations to account for the increased altitude should get you in the ballpark. Do not under-research the weather possibilities for your destination. You'll probably get a wide range of forecasts from these sources, so it's always a good idea to plan for the worst. It's far better to carry a few extra ounces for waterproof gear, an extra fleece, and ice axe than to cut corners and be exposed and in danger.

- **Temperature** dictates the amount and type of layering you bring to the mountains. Are you going to need thin soft-shell gloves, or thick Himalayan mitts? Will a 30-degree sleeping bag suffice, or will a negative-20-degree one be better at keeping you warm and alive?

  - Moisture management is the name of the game. If you're sweating, your clothing will be wet, and you'll need to be more aggressively addressing your hydration needs, and neither is optimal. Dressing in layers allows you to remove and add layers throughout the day as needed. And of course, all the layers should be synthetic or wool as these materials wick moisture away efficiently and keep you warm even when you're wet.

- There is an adage in the mountains: "Start cold." When you start out, avoid being bundled up with layers of down jackets, thick fleeces, hat, gloves, etc., especially if you will be ascending in short order. As soon as you start moving, you will generate heat. It's bound to happen – assess in real-time and remove a layer or two, but keep a wind-proof layer close at hand. If you begin hiking and then enter a shaded grove of pine trees and the temperature feels like it's dropping 10 degrees, then zip up your base layer, quickly throw your hat on, etc.

- If you'll be trekking in areas with snow or extreme cold, plan accordingly. Aside from hat, gloves, layers, sleeping bag, tent, etc., you should plan to bring two sleeping pads to keep the ice cold of your sleeping surface from sapping all the heat out of you: a closed-cell foam sleeping pad for the layer touching the ground or tent floor, and an inflatable Therm-a-Rest-style sleeping layer on top of that. One layer won't be enough.

- You'll also need to be aware of your hydration system. If it's freezing outside, it is common for your water bottle to freeze into a block of ice. If you use hydration pack, the hydration tube and bite valve will likely freeze solid. To counter this, keep your water bottles in the inside pockets of your jacket or an insulated receptacle. You can also buy neoprene sleeves that cover the hydration tubes to protect them from freezing.

- Batteries and electronics do not like extreme cold either. After you get back to your tent, put your critical electronics and battery powered devices into a spare pair of socks or insulated down mitts, and then put these inside your sleeping bag by your feet to keep them warm and operational through the night. This is another good reason to bring backup batteries (which also need to be protected in a warm environment!)

- Lastly, I wear contact lenses day-to-day at home and in the mountains. If you carry contact lenses, make sure they don't freeze overnight!

- **Altitude** influences temperature. You can estimate the temperature of your trek and camping locations with a simple formula: Take the reference temperature of your current location and subtract 3 degrees Fahrenheit for every 1000 vertical feet above that location (this may range to 5 degrees Fahrenheit for every 1000 feet in drier conditions). So, if your weather app indicates that the Ranger Station at 4,000 feet has a temperature of 45 degrees Fahrenheit, and your camp is at 9,000 feet, it will be 3 degrees X (5,000 vertical feet delta / 1,000 feet factor = 5) = 15 degrees colder at your camp = 30 degrees Fahrenheit approximate temperature.

Gear Essentials

While this is not an exhaustive list, here are some of the gear essentials for basic safety and survival on the mountain:

1) **Insulation** – the two primary insulation elements are what you choose to wear and the bag you choose to sleep in.
    a. **Clothing:** Layer with synthetic clothing to handle the worst potential conditions on the trek (e.g. snow, rain, wind, cold). A layered approach is optimal as it allows you to add and reduce layers to respond to the dynamic conditions throughout the day. A layering system should include:
        - A waterproof and breathable shell jacket,
        - An insulating layer (synthetic or wool fleece, synthetic or down fill – *note that you must keep down jackets dry, as they will lose loft and insulation capabilities when wet/moist*),
        - A base layer (synthetic or wool),
        - A hat or balaclava, and
        - Waterproof gloves.
    b. **Sleeping Bag and Sleeping Pad:** The **sleeping bag** is one of the "Big 3" items that will weigh the most during your trek. I recommend investing in a warm, yet lightweight sleeping bag made with modern, high-tech materials. There are two ways to go when selecting a sleeping bag for your trek: down or synthetic. A down sleeping bag is extremely lightweight and compresses very well. It's best for dry, cold environments. A synthetic sleeping bag does not compress as well and weighs more; however, if you will be in a potentially wet or moist environment, it's the only way to go. A **sleeping pad** will provide insulation from the cold ground, as well as cushioning from rocks, roots, and other

debris you may be sleeping on top of. Sleeping pads come in two primary forms, (1) closed-cell foam, and (2) self-inflating open-cell foam insulation. Avoid an air mattress constructed without built-in insulation – it will sap the heat right out of you. When sleeping on snow or ice, as mentioned, I recommend layering both a close-cell foam pad (on the ground), and a self-inflating open-cell foam pad on top of it. I've slept directly on snow before in a floorless tent, and this two-pad method worked perfectly and kept me comfortable all night.

2) **Shelter** – You'll need a tent (or a bivy sack if you're going the minimalist route), and absolutely bring an emergency blanket (a heat-reflecting body length material to wrap around yourself in an emergency) on your trek. Practice setting up and breaking down your tent so you can do it blindfolded. When you're at altitude, with

winds whipping over 40 mph, in the dark, in the middle of a rainstorm, the last thing you want is to be attempting to figure out how the tent goes together for the first time. The tent is another one of the "Big 3" items that will weigh the most during your trek – invest here in a strong yet lightweight tent with modern, high-tech materials. There are two primary types of tents: (1) a three-season tent made for excursions in spring, summer and autumn, comprised of a tent and rain fly with screen windows, and (2) a four-season tent made to handle the elements year-round.

3) **Nutrition and Hydration** –
   a. **Food:** Bring enough food to cover all the meals and snacks throughout the trek, and extra food in case of emergency. You'll need stove and fuel to heat up most meals. With dehydrated food, you will need to boil water to rehydrate the meal – plan your water accordingly. Your body burns a significant number of calories and processes proteins, carbohydrates, and fats differently when you're trekking 10 miles a day with a 50-pound pack on your back while at 10,000 feet elevation, versus if you're sitting in an office chair all day. Do some research in advance to learn what's right for you.
   b. **Water:** Bring a hydration bladder and/or water bottles, extra water, water purifier (pump or UV Light) or purifying tablets, and a stove and fuel to boil water to make it potable. You will need to replenish electrolytes; adding hydration tablets to your water bottle will help keep you thriving throughout the trek. Personally, I bring both a hydration

bladder and a water bottle: (1) I use the bladder during the trek to ensure I'm sipping water at the same rate that my body is processing it throughout the day (*as mentioned, the tube may freeze in cold weather; purchase a neoprene sleeve from the manufacturer to mitigate this*), and (2) I use the water bottle when purifying water as it's easier and more effective to do so if you're using a UV Light filter or tablets, I use this to fill the hydration bladder, and when done, I fill the water bottle back up and keep it as a backup if I or another member of the group runs out of water or needs extra water to prepare food, etc. Lastly, know where you can find water on your trekking route and be aware that certain times of the year water sources may dry up; this is a good question to ask the Park Ranger at the start of the trek.

4) **Fire** – You'll need waterproof matches, a lighter, or fire-starter. This is critical for boiling water and heating food. Most airlines will not let you bring lighters, fire starter, matches, or stove fuel on a plane. Plan to get these items in an outdoor adventure store near your trek location.

5) **Navigation and Communications** – A detailed map with elevation and trail distances, a compass, an altimeter watch, a GPS, a personal locator beacon, a cell phone and/or satellite phone, walkie-talkies, and backup batteries for all electronics are all essential. The altimeter watch is critical to not only assess altitude and time of day, but also measure barometric pressure, the ascent and descent rates of the climb, time of pace, etc.

6) **Illumination** – Invest in a good, bright, water-resistant headlamp and batteries. Pack additional batteries if an alpine start (night ascent) is part of the itinerary. And pack extra batteries just-in-case. A flashlight might be handy for base camp.
7) **First Aid Supplies and Hygiene** – In addition to standard first aid kit items and toiletries, be sure to add plenty of moleskin, a tick remover, and insect repellent. (*Note that insect repellent should contain DEET/Picaridin (avoid getting DEET on synthetic clothing, the harsh chemical known to cause damage to synthetic gear!), and clothing should be pre-treated with Permethrin. This is absolutely essential in an environment where mosquitos carry malaria or other viruses*). Include a hefty supply of baby wipes, hand sanitizer and camp soap – it gets dirty on those trails! Bring earplugs and a sleep mask if you want to ensure a good night's rest despite noisy camp neighbors or a snoring tent mate. If your vision is less than perfect, consider the trade-offs between wearing glasses (which may break) versus disposable contact lenses (which come with a potential for eye infections, and must be removed daily.) Some treks require to pack your waste out, so you may need to bring Restop Solid and Liquid Waste Bag, or you'll need a 6" trowel to dig and bury your waste. And don't forget toilet paper!

More on this "pack out waste" policy: it means you're literally packing out your poo and used TP. While nowadays you can buy solutions for this, when we climbed Mount Shasta, which had this policy, we made a homemade version of this solution comprised of a brown lunch-sized paper bag, filled with kitty litter, stored in zip lock, and then carried in an extra-strength-garbage-bag). As you can imagine, it takes a bit getting used to, and having THAT black extra-strength-garbage-bag strapped to your backpack makes for interesting trekking – one misstep and that big bag of poo could snag on a branch, tear on a narrow granite ledge, or worse!

8) **Tools and Repair Kit** – Bring a sharp sturdy knife, a multitool, duct tape, a tent repair kit, a whistle, signal device/mirror, etc. Airlines will require you to check-in your knife and multitool; you will not be able to carry it on the plane. Hopefully, you will not have to use any of these tools; however, hope is not a strategy, and these items will get you out of trouble when you're in a bind.

9) **Portage/Backpack** – This will protect your gear from the elements and will be worn on your back for hours and hours each day. The backpack is another of the "Big 3" items that will weigh the most during your trek, so plan to invest in a comfortable yet lightweight backpack with modern, high-tech materials.

- **Fit and Features** – Make sure to get a comfortable backpack that fits you well. You should be able to adjust the waist and shoulder straps to optimize load distribution and comfort. Look for features like hydration system holders, straps to compress the load, water proofing or rain cover, space to lash down ice axes or crampons, emergency whistle incorporated in the torso strap, zippered pouch to store valuables such as wallet and keys, etc.
- **Capacity** – Backpack capacity will be determined by the length of the trek as well as the season and expected conditions. For

example, a 10-day climb at high altitude during the winter will require a heck of a lot more gear and capacity than a day hike or an overnight hike in the summer would.

- **Weatherproofing your backpack** – There are 3 options:
    a) Recognize that your pack is not waterproof and use a big **contractor-grade garbage bag** as an overall insert to backpack, and use mini dry bags to protect your sleeping bag, down jacket, core clothing, sensitive electronic gear, etc. During my climb of Mount Kilimanjaro, I did not take this step and all of my gear was absolutely drenched when it down poured for hours on end; sleeping in wet clothes and a wet sleeping bag while attempting to use body heat to dry my clothing throughout the night. That's a mistake I will never make again!
    b) Use a backpack **rain cover**. This usually works very well to keep your backpack and its contents dry; however, while trekking in Patagonia, my trekking partner's rain cover blew completely off and flew down the mountain due to the 50 mph winds, despite being tightly secured to the pack. The key learning was to take the cover off or strap it even more securely in gale-force winds!
    c) Some gear companies are leveraging their **waterproof technologies** and incorporating them into their backpack lines. I now use Mountain Hardwear's OutDry backpack.
    d) **Test your backpack** – Prepare by fully loading your pack including water and food, and including what you'll have strapped to the outside, for example, trekking poles,

water bottles, etc. Does everything fit? How does the weight feel? Does it feel balanced or leaning to one side? Get out on the local trails and get comfortable with this heavy load in advance of your trek.

10) **Footwear System** – One of the most essential and important investments in the mountains is the shoes on your feet. It's absolutely vital to have a waterproof and breathable boot with solid ankle support so you can weather the elements. Expert Advice: Break in your boots long in advance of the trek. Start by wearing them around the house, then around town, and then wear them all day long (if your employer doesn't mind!), and of course head to the trails and break them in even more. You'll be living in these boots for 16-18 hours each day of your trek, both on the trail and around the camp – this is an investment you don't want to underfund.

a) **Trekking boots** – Look for boots that provide excellent support and are comparably very light weight so you're not being weighed down with each step. As you may not be able to afford the incremental weight of camp shoes, make sure these boots are ultra-comfortable. I use the Salomon Quest 4D 3 GTX hiking boots.

b) **Mountaineering boots** – When mountaineering and traversing snow and ice with crampons, you need a more hard-core boot with an extremely rigid steel shank, so the crampons stay attached. I use the La Sportiva Nepal EVO Gore-Tex mountaineering boots.

c) **Footbed Inserts** – I highly recommend upgrading the footbed inserts to orthotics like SuperFeet. Critical note here: There's a difference between the different insert models that each manufacturer sells; there are models for low-arch feet and others for high-arch feet. I mistakenly grabbed the high-arch inserts and my feet were in excruciating pain before even getting into the mountains.

d) **Socks** – I recommend using a system of two layers of socks: a polypropylene thin base layer and a thick synthetic or wool second layer. Any friction will occur between these two layers, thereby keeping the skin on the soles of your feet where it belongs!

e) **Feet protection** – I apply Band-Aid Friction Block stick each morning as well. Some trekkers use moleskin, while others use duct tape if blisters are emerging. Carefully monitor feet all day for hotspots and address immediately.

f) **Gaiters** – Essential for keeping scree, pebbles or snow from getting into your boots.

g) **Extra shoelaces** – I'd recommend keeping an extra pair of laces in your repair kit for multi-day treks, in case one breaks.

11) **Trekking Poles** – I find trekking poles essential as I've had three knee surgeries over the years. However, you don't have to have knee issues to find trekking poles useful. They provide stability, can be used as brakes on the descent to spare your knees, and enable you to use your upper body to help you accelerate on climbs and flat terrain. They're also extremely useful if your terrain requires

snowshoes. Definitely get the rubber tips to prevent the poles from tearing your other gear when not in use and get the snow baskets if you'll be traversing snow.

12) **Sun protection** – Absolutely essential. Pack sunglasses and/or glacier glasses, sunscreen, lip balm, and a good-quality hat.

13) **Other Adventure-Specific Gear** – As you research the terrain and environment that you'll be traversing, you may discover you'll need specific gear for that environment:

(a) **Snow territory** – Bring an ice axe, crampons, ropes, avalanche beacon, goggles, and snowshoes if you're planning to be in snow country. Be aware that while crampons and snowshoes may feel tight at base camp, they loosen up as you start moving. Be sure to readjust after several minutes of climbing, and periodically at rest stops after that. Loose snowshoes are less efficient, but loose crampons are dangerous.

(b) **Canyon territory** – Bring canyoneering boots and a long sturdy wooden pole if you're planning to be in canyon country.

(c) **Snake territory** – Bring a snake bite kit if you'll be in an area known for dangerous snakes.

(d) **Bear territory** – Lock up or hang all your food and anything scented (toothpaste, toothbrush, deodorant, soap, hand sanitizer, sun screen, lip balm, everything!), and if you're in an area with permanently fixed bear lockers, put everything inside as soon as you arrive and lock the door immediately. Years ago, while settling into camp in Yosemite Valley, we made sure we were very thorough about putting everything in the bear locker. We started talking and got distracted for a moment, forgetting to lock the locker; the next thing we knew there was a 400-pound bear pulling all the food out of the locker and gorging on everything a mere five feet away from us.

Again, worth noting that most airlines will not allow fire supplies/ starters, stoves, or fuel on board the aircraft for safety reasons, so you'll likely need to plan to get these when you arrive. Also be aware of what you can check-in versus carry on board. You will not be able to carry on-board your knife or multitool, and some airlines don't like trekking poles, ice axes, and crampons carried on the aircraft, but they're okay to check-in. Please check the airline's guidelines in advance to avoid surprises and plan accordingly for what you may need to acquire as soon as you arrive.

Gear Inspection and Humiliation

There's a delicate balance between carrying every possible item that you can possibly use versus Traveling Light/Traveling Right. I had an eye-opener at the start of our Mount Shasta mountaineering trip. Definitely a coachable moment for me! The morning of the trek we were told to meet the climbing guides in the Mountain Adventure Seminars parking lot. We were instructed lay out all our gear on the ground, so everything was exposed for the Guides to assess.

They were testing two things:
> *(1) Did we follow the instructions and pack all the essential items they directed us to bring?*
> *(2) Did we bring only the essential gear?*

So, it was a bit humiliating to hear a guide say, "Do you really need five pairs of socks and six pairs of underwear for a three-day climb?!" The point was to bring only the gear you NEED, and only as much clothing as you could comfortably wear all at the same time. The embarrassment ensured I'd never forget the lesson! Being weighed down by 15 pounds of non-essential gear and luxury items makes you less likely to be successful in the summit attempt, and more likely to be a liability if moving rapidly up or down the mountain becomes critical.

Temperature and Moisture Management
While I mentioned this earlier, it's worth highlighting again that constantly monitoring your body temperature is essential in the mountains. Sweating is not just uncomfortable; it also increases your water consumption. We learned on Mount Shasta to "start cold," meaning even though you might be freezing at the start the trek/climb, once you start moving you will rapidly generate heat. It's best to adjust your clothing *before* you start, in anticipation of the temperature your body will be once you're on the move.

Ultra-Light Gear versus Fitness
An admittedly fun habit is to monitor gear companies' releases of new products each year, as captured in various outdoor magazine annual gear guides and ongoing gear reviews throughout the year. It's great to see how technology and innovation solve the challenges experienced by everyone who spends time in the mountains. There is a strong pull to be constantly upgrading as gear gets lighter, stronger,

and more functional each year. Once it sinks in that all that gear that you've got in your backpack must be carried over dozens and dozens of miles up and down thousands of feet of elevation, having ultralight gear and shaving ounces off of everything becomes an obsession.

That said, a critical factor in saving weight ties back to Cardiovascular Strength. A lightbulb went off as I was trying to find the lightest (yet warmest) sleeping bag that would shave a huge 8 ounces off the weight totals, ignoring the fact that I had somehow allowed 10 extra pounds of body weight to creep up on me over the previous 12 months of less-than-perfect nutrition and virtually no cardiovascular training!

Part of your preparation plan should be to get to a more ideal body weight before the climb begins. A friend who has begun training for a summit attempt of Mount Rainier told me was hitting the local trails wearing a weighted training vest to get into shape for the climb. He commented that hiking with 20 pounds in the vest was exhausting. It's the same as carrying 20 pounds of excess body weight. Proper weight loss takes time, so if needed, don't wait to start right-sizing.

Contingency Planning

Contingency planning is paramount. Not only will it save time and mental energy on the trek; it may very well save you from injury (or worse). Some scenarios to consider:

- What if a route is impassible due to snow, rockfall, or flooding?
- What if a critical piece of gear fails, as it did for us in Tahoe when our floorless tent collapsed in the heavy snow?

- What if your primary water source has dried up or is contaminated?
- What if you forget a key piece of gear, such as a head lamp or a rain fly for the tent?
- What if you plan for heat and it starts raining or snowing?
- What if you get lost? Or injured? Or encounter a bear? Or your batteries die? Or your group gets split up?

As they say in the Navy Seals, "Two is one, one is none." Bring redundant gear, and plan for everything.

(Flattened tent due to flash snowstorm dumping over three feet of snow in three hours.)

Every Ounce Counts – <u>Excerpt from Appendix C:</u> Julius (our lead guide up Mount Kilimanjaro) was clear with me that I was moving too slowly. He said, "Stop here. Don't question me." I'm thinking, "oh no, this is it – he's going to pull me from the climb". However, when I stop, he removes the two Nalgene water bottles attached to my summit pack. That's about a half-gallon of water weighing around 4 pounds. It's incredible what a huge difference 4 pounds makes. I have a total of 5 liters of water with me; in retrospect, it's too much. Cutting corners on water is risky; however, for this specific summit night it's a non-issue, and it's helping me a ton to be relieved of this weight. Julius and Godfrey are each carrying one of my Nalgene bottles to the top of the mountain for me. I'm really glad Julius stopped me, and I immediately begin moving at a healthy pace.

Synthetic Gear – <u>Excerpt from Appendix C:</u> So, you're probably wondering, "If all your gear was absolutely soaked yesterday in that massive rainstorm (when making the approach on New Shira camp on Mount Kilimanjaro) how did you survive the night?" There an expression in the mountains, "Cotton Kills". Yes, everything was drenched, however all my clothing and my sleeping bag were synthetic. While it doesn't dry automatically, it will keep you warm when wet. So, all night long I was up, changing into wet clothes, using my body heat to dry it throughout the night, and changing again repeating this manual drying process. While I missed much-needed sleep, through this process I was able to expand my selection of dry clothes from just a couple pieces of clothing, to drying most of the critical clothing and gear elements. Really, it was successful night!

The Value of Illumination – <u>Excerpt from Appendix C:</u> I knew at this stage there were only a couple hours before daylight as we were making our final push to the summit of Mount Kilimanjaro – I started thinking yes, I'm tired, but what I really need is the light to wake up the brain. I felt when daylight hit, not only would it warm up this frigid air, but it would wake up the mind and body and give me that extra boost I could use for the summit. Also, when I had turned off that headlamp earlier, not only was I mis-stepping more, but the darkness was adding to my feeling of sleepiness. Light was going to be the solution, and I was going to get the headlamp fired back up right away. After finally finding the replacement batteries, and with help installing them in the headlamp with frozen fingers, the beam was bright, really bright – it gave me the added boost I needed!

Alcohol and Yak Meat – <u>Excerpt from Appendix B:</u> Gorak Shep Lodge: Interesting night tonight. There was a group of trekkers that arrived in the dining area about the same time we did. They were a lively bunch and were really enjoying a couple rounds of Nepalese beer. As the Sherpa people revere the mountains as sacred, I did not partake in alcohol while on the mountain (I also knew it would interfere with acclimatization which was another compelling reason to abstain for the few days we were in the mountains). This group also was brave and ordered the yak stew for dinner. Since the start of the trek, I stuck to a predominately vegetarian and eggs diet and avoided meat for two reasons: the locals are primarily vegetarians and more importantly, during the day of trekking up the mountain, we'd see Sherpa porters with slabs of yak meat strapped to their backs, heading up to the lodges to supply them with meat for the tourist trekkers. This was completely unrefrigerated on their backs for hours in the sun as the porters climbed up the mountain, and if that's not enough we'd frequently see swarms of flies buzzing around the porters' yak meat as they'd pass us climbing up the trail. Simple math said, "Avoid the meat at all costs!!" Unfortunately, these trekkers did not see what we did or chose to ignore it, and in the middle of the night we heard every one of them racing to the bathroom and moaning in pain as they had competing diarrhea and vomiting all night. Unfortunately, our room was right next to the bathroom and we heard it all through those paper-thin Tea Hut walls — all night long. We honestly were afraid that the raw sewage and vomit would be seeping into our room from the overflowing mess they made in the bathroom.

Trail Animals and Tourists — <u>Excerpt from Appendix B:</u> Sometimes a trekking day with no tourists and no yaks to contend with is a great day.

    First, while it's great to meet like-minded adventurers trekking to a common destination, at altitude I found that I'd rather be where it's a bit more remote so that we're not dealing with tourists' loud chatter late into the night or early morning disturbing our precious sleep. Also, tons-of-tourists leads to tons-of-congestion on the trails/tea houses, making everything slow and negatively impacting progress to the daily arrival goals.

    Second, yaks are incredible animals, which somehow have adapted to a world with very little oxygen in the air. They are absolutely critical to enable trekkers and climbers to have a chance to make it to their destination, and also enable the tea houses to stock their business so they can make a living as well. That said, aside from dodging endless yak dung for miles and miles on the trail, it's a bit nerve-racking as you're passing the yaks trekking to your destination for the day. First many times the trails are very narrow, and just barely etched into the walls in the mountain; sometimes just wide enough for you to pass with a 1000-foot drop if you make a mistake and don't watch your step. It seemed like every tight spot on the trail, there would be a group of yaks, loaded with gear they are carrying up the mountain, trying to squeeze by on that same bit of narrow trail. I can't count how many times I thought I would get bumped into and either drop 1000 feet to my untimely death or get crushed against the rock wall on the other side of the narrow trail. Also, there are many long rickety suspension bridges crossing large valleys and rivers along the trek. Even if another trekker or two are walking on the bridge, the thing is bouncing around and creaking from the strain. Add the normal winds whipping down these valleys and it's a white knuckler! Then, inevitably, when you halfway across, somehow there's a fully loaded yak heading right towards you. In cases like this, there's no mountain wall to be smashed against — it's a 1000 foot drop on either side into a rocky and icy racing Himalayan river born from the snow melt of these massive peaks watching over head.

Preparation: Lodging selection — Choose the Highest Lodge —
<u>Excerpt from Appendix B:</u> *Raj seems to take us to the highest lodge in the highest part of every village — we did that in Namche, Pangboche,*

and after no vacancy in the first few lodges in Dingboche, Chris and I (apparently to Raj's dismay) pushed for the highest lodge again!!

We felt it was a good strategy to get a couple hundred extra more vertical feet elevation for sleep (to aid acclimatization) and also, in the morning, you skip the congestion of the trekkers in the village.

Preparation: Locking Down Lodging in Advance – _Excerpt from Appendix B:_ On the Everest Base Camp trek, half of me is a little frustrated that each day we are searching for lodging and that it wasn't locked in before we even stepped foot on the mountain. We risk not having a place to stay, which is what happened to Tengboche a couple days earlier. We did not have tents – only sleeping bags – so, while we could have bivouacked in an emergency (albeit illegally), it was risky as at any moment a storm could blow in and dump snow and heavy winds on us. In every other major trek that I've done, precise logistics are essential, and reservations for permits, campsites, lodging, etc. had to be done months in advance. We were nervous, especially during the current Himalayan high season, we might be left out in the cold.

That said, the other half of me likes how we we're able to customize the trek on the fly. We cut out that Tengboche day and decided to do the Chukhung Ri pass route and cut out another day. We couldn't have done this if the lodging/routing had been set in stone. It's a balance, and, so far we've been lucky.

This picture is from Mount Whitney, 1997, my first major trek at over 14,000 feet, as described in Appendix A. I learned a lot on this trip. I was wearing cotton army pants, rigid leather combat boots, with a cotton bandana, and I'm standing next to my buddy's $20 budget tent. While we survived, we learned a number of important lessons, and a lot of the preparation and gear would change and be upgraded over the years to follow.

> *"There are no secrets to success. It is the result of preparation, hard work, and learning from failure."*
> *– Colin Powell*

SAMPLE GEAR LIST

....

"I am prepared for the worst but hope for the best."
– Benjamin Disraeli

Here is a sample list of gear for my Teton Crest Trail trek in the Grand Tetons National Park in Wyoming; late September to early October time frame; at high elevation around 10,000 feet; with temperatures ranging from 15 degrees Fahrenheit (nighttime low temperatures) to 65 degrees Fahrenheit (daytime high temperatures).

It should be noted that gear companies are constantly evolving their product lines, introducing stronger, lighter, and more feature-rich and capable gear each year. While this list worked for me at the time, you need to assess your wants versus needs based on your budget for the adventure. My advice is safety comes first, and with gear as your main defense versus the elements and everything that Mother Nature can throw at you, do not be excessively frugal with this investment.

Disclaimer: While many products are referenced in this book, the author does not receive any compensation from the manufacturers for their reference.

☒	CATEGORY	DESCRIPTION
☐	Backpack	Osprey Variant 52 Backpack (52 liter), with Osprey 100 oz Hydration Bladder
☐	Sleeping Bag	Mountain Hardwear Phantom 0 Degree Down Sleeping Bag
☐	Sleeping Pad	Therm-a-Rest ProLite 4 Regular & Stuff Sack
☐	Sleeping Pad	Therm-a-Rest Lite Seat (doubles as a pillow)
☐	Tent	Mountain Hardwear Direkt2 Tent & Footprint (Ueli Steck gear line)
☐	Ice Axe	Corsa Camp Ultralight Ice Axe w/ leash
☐	Crampons	Kahtoola Micro-spikes
☐	Trekking Poles	Black Diamond Z Pole Carbon Ultralight
☐	Boots	Salomon GTX Boots w/ SuperFeet
☐	Outer Shell	Mountain Hardwear Quasar DryQ Ultralight Waterproof/Breathable Pullover Jacket (Ueli Steck gear line) - State Orange
☐	Outer Shell	Mountain Hardwear Quasar DryQ Ultralight Waterproof/Breathable Pant (Ueli Steck gear line) - Shark
☐	Outer Shell	Mountain Hardwear Hooded Ghost Whisperer Ultralight 800 Down Jacket
☐	Gloves	Mountain Hardwear HydraPro Waterproof Gloves (Ueli Steck gear line)
☐	Hat	Mountain Hardwear Zerna Beanie (Ueli Steck gear line)
☐	Stuff Sack	Sea-to-Summit 13 Liter UltraSil Stuff Sack - Orange
☐	Gear	Suunto Advizor Altimeter Watch & HRM
☐	Hat	REI Softshell (Baseball) Hat
☐	Outer Layer	Mountain Hardwear Densa Hoodie Fleece (Ueli Steck gear line) - State Orange
☐	Outer Layer	Mountain Hardwear Warlow Softshell Pants (Ueli Steck gear line) - Shark
☐	Belt	Mountain Hardwear Nut Belt - Black
☐	Base Layer	Mountain Hardwear Elmoro S/S Shirt (Ueli Steck gear line) - Black

[X] CATEGORY	DESCRIPTION
☐ Base Layer	Mountain Hardwear Wicked Lite L/S Shirt - Black
☐ Base Layer	Mountain Hardwear Wicked Lite L/S Shirt - Titanium
☐ Base Layer	Patagonia Capilene 2 Long Underwear - Grey
☐ Base Layer	EMS Synthetic Boxer Briefs
☐ Socks	Smartwool PhD Medium Crew Socks - Black
☐ Socks	Silver Sock Liners (x2)
☐ Stuff Sack	Sea-to- Summit 8 Liter UltraSil Stuff Sack - Green
☐ Gear	Steripen Adventurer Opti UV Water Purifier w/ Extra Battery (Energizer CR123) & Pre-Filter
☐ Gear	Princeton Tec Remix Headlamp w/ Extra Batteries (Lithium Energizer AAA x3) & Petzl Case
☐ Gear	Camp Nano 23 Wire Carabiner
☐ Gear	MSR Packtowel - Small - Blue
☐ Stuff Sack	Sea-to- Summit 2 Liter UltraSil Stuff Sack - Green
☐ Gear	Adventure Medical Kits - Pocket Survival Pack
☐ Gear	Adventure Medical Kits - Emergency Blanket
☐ Gear	Wenger Titanium Professional Mountaineer Ueli Steck Knife/Multi-Tool w/ carrying case & 3 screw bits
☐ Gear	Gerber Bear Grills Folding Knife
☐ Gear	SealLine Waterproof iPhone Case
☐ Gear	Sunglasses & Sunglasses Case
☐ Stuff Sack	Sea-to-Summit 4 Liter UltraSil Stuff Sack - Orange
☐ Electronics	Panasonic Lumix DMC-ZS10 16x Optical Zoom Full HD Camera w/ 3 batteries, 32gb SDHC card, and Charger
☐ Electronics	iPhone w/ Bumper, headset w/ mic, charger & cable, car charger
☐ Gear	Backpackers Cache Bear Canister

The Seven Strengths of Summiting | **Mark Santino**

☒	CATEGORY	DESCRIPTION
☐	Food	Freeze Dried Food x3
☐	Food	Energy Bars x 8, 2 Cheez-Its, 1 bag peanuts
☐	Food	CamelBak Electrolytes x3
☐	Gear	Water Bottle
☐	Gear	Ultra-Light Camp Stove, Ceramic 16 oz mug w/ GSI Outdoors Silicon Gripper
☐	Gear	Bear Bell
☐	Gear	Counter Assault Canister Holder & Canister
☐	Gear	Medical Kit incl Pain Medicine, Benadryl, Vitamins
☐	Gear	Toiletries Kit incl Bugspray, Iodine Tabs, Sunscreen
☐	Gear	Wipes, TP, Sanitizer

The Seven Strengths of Summiting | **Mark Santino**

(Gear organized and ready to go for the next trek!)

THE JOURNEY IS THE DESTINATION

"If you cannot understand that there is something in man which responds to the challenge of this mountain and goes out to meet it, that the struggle is the struggle of life itself upward and forever upward, then you won't see why we go."
– Sir Edmund Hillary

Why Climb/Trek?

"Why do you climb?" Back in the day, I used to respond to that question as George Mallory did: "Because it is there!" But that answer never really satisfies the inquirer. Every person who spends time in the mountains will have a different response. The real answers for me are:

- The view from the top, and especially the extraordinary views during the route to the top.
- The challenge – pushing oneself to achieve something difficult and learning about oneself in the process.
- The cultural immersion/enlightenment and the people you meet along the way.
- The tranquility of mountain life – free from the day-to-day grind and stressors, free from the man-made pollutions, free from the constant buzz of the always-on digital world we live in.
- The ability to bond and communicate at a more profound level with the friends you are traveling with.
- Hitting the refresh button and being ready to take on the world and all its challenges when you get back to civilization.
- At the core of it, the journey is the destination!

Use of Guides/Porters

There's a healthy debate about getting to the summit unaided versus having porters carrying all your gear. (*First, you're always carrying a day pack, so you're never carrying nothing.*) Definitely hotly contested. It's your choice, of course; however, I personally recommend using local guides/porters. My rationale:

- **Give**: For many of these folks, your trek is their primary source of income – you're helping them put food on the table or improve their livelihood. You're certainly getting a bargain using local help, so I suggest taking a chunk of the money saved from not going with a premium firm and giving your guides or porters a massive tip.
- **Culture:** As I've already mentioned, using local guides and porters allows you to interact with more locals and learn about their culture.
- **Be inspired:** Hear them laugh and sing in their native language, lifting your spirits.
- **Be amazed:** While you're huffing and puffing with 25 pounds in your little day pack, they're flying ahead of you on the trail in flip-flops with 50 pounds balanced on their head or back. You'll notice the crew quietly waits for you to leave camp before breaking down your tent and packing up everything, and then in no time, they're passing you on the trail. And by the time you reach the next camp, the tents are already set up, the water is purified, and dinner is ready!
- **Learn:** during our trip to Everest Base Camp we had one guide and one porter. We stayed at tea houses along the route, so the porter's load was "light", but our diminutive Sherpa still carried 50+ pounds on his back. What was amazing was watching him trek. While I was staring at the scenery and stumbling over rocks on the trail, he took short, even paces with very precise foot placement with every step and avoided every single pebble on the trail. In this way, he

conserved energy, avoided the wear and tear on his feet, and moved effortlessly through the mountains. He routinely arrived at the next camp ahead of us, even if he left after we did. Heck, this is what he does for a living — he's put in his 10,000 hours. Observe and learn from everyone along the way.

> **"In every walk with nature one receives far more than he seeks."**
> *— John Muir*

Leave No Trace

This is a common warning sign that you see at most trailheads. It means, buy souvenirs, make friends, get contact info from the people you meet, and take all the photos you want. Just leave the environment as you found it, or cleaner/better (for example, by picking up trash). Don't take the mountain back home with you.

Be Flexible

There's a balance between sticking to the detailed plan and being flexible and open to some 'game day' options. So, let's say you move briskly with purpose and free up a day, maybe you can go home a day early and surprise the family, or fit in an extra day hike out to a stunning waterfall. Or, it might be a balance of living in a tent for a week versus grabbing a hotel room for a night: Take a well-earned shower, spend a night with the locals at a pub, eat local food versus yet another freeze-dried meal, etc. It's all about flexibility and balance.

Be Open to Serendipity

We were virtually out of gas, as we were driving back from Patagonia National Park and heading to El Calafate, Argentina. There is one gas station between the Patagonia in Chile and El Calafate. It was a miracle — we actually made it back to town coasting and the car was literally driving on fumes. To make a rough day a little rougher, all the hotels were completely booked in the town. So, we drove in the direction of the next National Park, hoping to find place to pull over and camp. After miles and miles of driving, we decided to take a left and drove 2 miles down this dirt road. It was the middle of the night and we were wiped out and had no idea if the road was going to get us anywhere. We pulled over on the side of the road and decided to just sleep in the car. We were not in a legal parking area, but we thought because we were just going to nod off in the car and not set up a tent, if the authorities asked us to keep moving, we could just drive out of the area quickly. After all that driving, I needed to relieve myself. I got out of the car and just I happened to glance up. What I saw next was the most incredible star scenery I have ever seen in my entire life. It literally looked like I could touch the stars – like they bowed in on this part of earth and we were exponentially closer. The pitch darkness from a perfectly clear, moonless night was extraordinary; I was literally able to see an ultra-high definition view of the Milky Way. Words cannot describe – I could see what looked like a black hole – a pure black circle, smack-dab in the middle of the Milky Way, and a billion high-definition stars around it. So, what could have turned out to be a major inconvenience of running out of gas in the middle of nowhere, turned into one of the most extraordinary nights ever.

When the Trek is Over

Trekking is absolutely exhilarating, yet immensely challenging at the same time. When you do get back to the trail head or back to civilization, it's essential to:

- Compare notes.
- Laugh and celebrate – you've earned it.
- Reminisce about what was tough, what was extraordinary, what should be done differently next time.

- Call home and let them know you're ok and safely out of the mountains.
- Share pictures and stories with family and friends.
- And most importantly, begin to talk about your next adventure: What are your top three destination options? When would the next adventure be? (It's worth noting that this is a topic you may want to avoid when you're on day 3 of a 15-day trek with 90 brutal miles of trekking uphill in front of you, perhaps with altitude sickness symptoms, your stomach unsettled from what you ate or drank in the village before the trek began, with your feet killing you, your shoulders and back sore from weight of the pack, insects relentlessly biting you, the sun beating down on you (or rain pouring on you, or snow up to your waist), sleep deprived, etc. Trust me, wait just a little bit longer – maybe wait until you're approaching the parking lot or diving into that well-earned slice of pizza, before broaching the subject. You'll definitely get more takers!

"Keep climbing to your own life's summits."
– Jim Whittaker

The Seven Strengths of Summiting | **Mark Santino**

The Seven Strengths of Summiting | **Mark Santino**

CONCLUSION

....

"It is not the mountain we conquer but ourselves."
— Sir Edmund Hillary

So, you get the picture now. It's all about balance. It's about self-awareness, situational awareness, emotional awareness. It's about preparation – environmentally, physically and mentally. It's about being open to what you will experience – the good and the less good. The journey in the mountains, as in life, is the destination.

I thought about what I would tell my 20-year-old self if I could go back in time. My advice would be:
- The Journey is the Destination.
- Dream big – what would you love to see or do, regardless of how bold it is?
- Create a bucket list. It truly is amazing how time flies. You need a plan to achieve goals.
- Invest in more in experiences and less in stuff.
- Be open to serendipity – don't micro-plan everything (but still plan close to everything!)
- Explore/trek more – get outside more.
- Expand the net – try to get more people to join you to share the experience.
- Force my kids to come with me on trips even when they say no!
- Give back more, especially the communities you adventure in.
- Learn another language.
- Be sure to balance buddy-adventures with family-adventures.

The Seven Strengths of Summiting | **Mark Santino**

> *"Physical strength (hard work), mental strength (perseverance) and spiritual strength (love and acceptance) are the keys to continuous growth."*
> *– Rickson Gracie*

The lightbulb went off for me while trekking to Mount Everest Base Camp, that there are seven inter-related strengths to find success in the mountains. Without a doubt, preparation is the key to success. Don't let the first time you're stuck in the rain or snow be on the slopes of Mount Kilimanjaro at 16,000. Start small and work your way up to the big mountains, accumulating experience as you go. The more physical and cardio preparation you do, the more time spent with your climbing team, the more time getting comfortable with your gear and pushing forward through adversity, the more your overall whole-person strength and confidence will increase, and your chances of success will soar. Have a blast and climb on!

"So, which mountain are we going to climb next?!..."

The Seven Strengths of Summiting | **Mark Santino**

BONUS CHAPTER:
THE SEVEN STRENGTHS OF SUMMITING IN BUSINESS

"The will to win, the desire to succeed, the urge to reach your full potential... these are the keys that will unlock the door to personal excellence"
— Confucius

After over 25 years of business and leadership experience, I've learned that being successful in business also requires not just one single strength, but seven complementary and interconnected strengths. I will highlight them here briefly and expand in a subsequent book.

The Seven Strengths of Summiting in Business are:

- **Intellectual Strength**: This strength includes technical acumen, requiring a commitment to continuously sharpening the intellectual saw to keep your skillset current and evolve as the market and technology evolves; ongoing learning is imperative as is the ability to adapt and respond to the way the world is in reality, not the way you wish it would be.

- **Emotional Strength**: Emotional intelligence is crucial, as are self-awareness and self-control; true leadership is borne from passion, positivity, and a realistically optimistic outlook. The best leaders never "phone in" their performance; they are always passionately present in the moment for their teams and for the business.

- **Mental Strength:** This strength includes a results-and-achievement orientation, perseverance and the will to win, diligence, the ability to battle adversity, effective conflict management, adaptability and an aptitude for driving change, dedication to the mission, intense focus with the capacity to eliminate distractions, visualizing success at a high stakes meeting or presentation, and the pursuit of an optimal work-life blend (with the understanding that a true balance is unachievable).

- **Preparation and Prioritization Strength:** Working smarter is the focus of this strength: Investing significant time in planning and preparation, as well as prioritizing and triage; having the confidence and conviction to say "no" when necessary; having a stop-start-continue approach at all times; continuously assessing what is core to the strategy of the business versus low-impact context and having the discipline to optimize accordingly; focusing on the right things at the right time to give the organization a competitive advantage; planning and dedicating the time and resources necessary for continual improvement; changing before you have to; setting stretch and super stretch goals, with the understanding that you cannot achieve unless you dream big.

- **Communication Strength:** Effective business communicators are crisp and direct in their delivery; they tell it like it is. As listeners, they are present in the moment and are actively engaged (we were born with two ears and one mouth, take the lead from nature). They understand that preparation is key to all important communications and that maintaining the alignment of verbal and non-verbal communication is critical.

- **Collaboration Strength:** Strong leaders are able to set aside their ego and put the team first. They empower their people to drive the business with their customers at heart and hold them accountable for their decisions. They embody the adage that you win together, and you lose together. They excel at managing challenging performance. To this end, they invest time and effort in coaching and mentoring, spending more of their time with the top performers. They promote a culture of inclusion and diversity throughout the team, a relentless customer and shareholder focus, and a conviction that people are a company's greatest assets.

- **The "Greater Good" Strength:** This includes understanding and embodying your "why"; fulfilling on multiple levels; giving back (as team!); making a positive impact on society (Corporate Social Responsibility); and baking ethics and integrity into everything you do and say.

Similar to the Seven Strengths of Summiting mountains, these Business Strengths are all intertwined – each strength complements and augments the others. This is the only way to reach the summit in business.

"Choose a job you love, and you will never have to work a day in your life."
– Confucius

RECOMMENDED READING

Great Books to Inform and Inspire:
A. *Mountaineering – Freedom of the Hills* by The Mountaineers
B. *A Life on The Edge* by Jim Whittaker
C. *Endurance – Shackleton's Incredible Voyage* by Alfred Lansing
D. *Mission Possible – A Decade of Living Dangerously* by Ash Dykes
E. *Travels* by Michael Crichton

The Seven Strengths of Summiting | **Mark Santino**

APPENDICES

Trekking Logs:
    A. Mount Whitney (1997)
    B. Everest Base Camp (2004)
    C. Mount Kilimanjaro (2007)

These appendices are essentially stream-of-consciousness travelogues scribbled in notebooks from three notable treks at altitude, each trek being personally enlightening in its own way. These experiences shaped the core of this book and the genesis of my thoughts on how to accelerate preparation before embarking upon one's first big mountain. Clearly the rarified air plays a role in my frame of mind and commentary in the following! Reader beware!

The Seven Strengths of Summiting | **Mark Santino**

The Seven Strengths of Summiting | **Mark Santino**

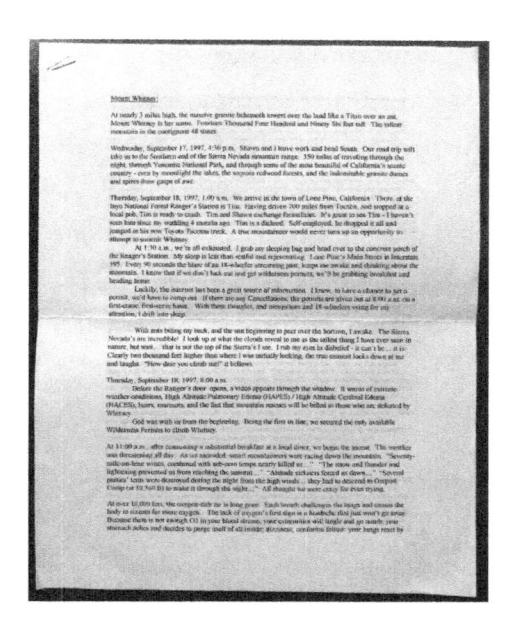

APPENDIX A:
MOUNT WHITNEY (1997)

....

At nearly 3 miles high, the massive granite behemoth towers over the land like a Titan over an ant. Mount Whitney is her name. Fourteen Thousand Four Hundred and Ninety-Six feet tall: The tallest mountain in the contiguous 48 states.

Wednesday, September 17, 1997, 4:30 pm:

Shawn and I leave work and head South. Our road trip will take us to the southern end of the Sierra Nevada mountain range. 350 miles of traveling through the night, through the Yosemite National Park, and through some of the most beautiful of California's scenic country – even by moonlight, the lakes, the sequoia redwood forests, and the indomitable granite domes and spires draw gasps of awe.

Thursday, September 18, 1997, 1:00 am:

We arrive in the town of Lone Pine, California. There at the Inyo National Forest's Ranger's Station is Tim. Having driven 700 miles from Tucson, and stopped at a local pub, he's ready to crash. It's great to see him – the last time was at my wedding 4 months ago. Tim is a diehard: Self-employed, he dropped it all and jumped into his new Toyota Tacoma truck. A true mountaineer would never turn down an opportunity to attempt to summit Whitney.

At 1:30 am, we're all exhausted. I grab my sleeping bag and head over to the concrete porch of the Ranger's Station. My sleep is less than restful. Lone Pine's Main Street is Interstate 395. Every 90 seconds the blare of an 18-wheeler screaming past keeps me awake and thinking about the mountain. I know that if we don't luck out and get wilderness permits, we'll be grabbing breakfast and heading home.

Luckily, the internet has been a great source of information. We knew, to have a chance to get a permit, we'd have to camp out overnight at the Ranger's Station. If there are any cancellations, the permits are given out at 8:00 am on a first-come, first-served basis. With those thoughts and mosquitos and 18-wheelers vying for my attention, I drift into sleep.

I awake to ants biting my back, and the sun beginning to peer over the horizon. The Sierra Nevada Mountains are incredible! I look up at what the clouds reveal to me as the tallest thing I have ever seen in nature — but wait… that's not the top of the Sierras I see. I rub my eyes in disbelief — it can't be… It is! Clearly two thousand feet higher than where I was initially looking, the true summit looks down at me and laughs. "How dare you climb me!" it bellows.

Thursday, September 18, 1997, 8:00 am:

Before the Ranger's door opens, my attention is caught by a news report I can see through the station window. It warns of extreme weather conditions, High Altitude Pulmonary Edema (HAPE)/ High Altitude Cerebral Edema (HACE), bears, marmots, and the fact that mountain rescues will be billed to those defeated by Whitney.

We're very fortunate; being the first in line, we secured the only available wilderness permits to climb Whitney.

At 11:00 am, we have a substantial breakfast at a local diner. I always eat way too much at these pre-climb-local-diner-breakfasts — you'd think it was my last supper. The overeating ultimately weighs me down (nothing like burping up breakfast as you rapidly gain altitude trekking), and then needing to purge the brick in your stomach several hours later!).

We begin our ascent. The weather has been threatening all day and smart mountaineers are racing down the mountain. "Seventy-mile-an-hour winds, combined with sub-zero temps nearly killed us…"; "The snow and thunder and lightning kept us from reaching the summit…"; "Altitude sickness forced us down…"; "Several parties' tents were destroyed the night before from the high winds… they had to descend to Outpost Camp (at 10,360 feet) to make it through the night…"

Everyone we speak with thinks we're crazy for even trying. Maybe they're right! At over 10,000 feet, the oxygen-rich air is long gone. Each breath challenges the lungs and causes the body to scream for more oxygen. The first sign of lack of oxygen is a headache that just won't go away. Because there's not enough O_2 in your bloodstream, your extremities will tingle and go numb; your stomach aches and decides to purge itself; dizziness and confusion follow; your lungs react by filling with fluid (HAPE) and you slowly drown in your own edema; your brain does the same; once it swells, certain death is eminent.

At about 11,000 feet, the mist — which has turned to rain — decides it's too cold to remain in a liquid form, and it begins to snow. The wind has picked up considerably. 35 mile-an-hour gusts make each step with a 52-pound pack even tougher. Altitude has magnified the weigh on my back. Every step consists of a deep breath, a brush of snow off my face and a draining climb to higher elevation. We passed the tree-line long ago — no protection from the elements exists, except for adrenalin and the Gore-Tex covering my torso.

At 12,039 feet, we arrive at our base camp, called Trail Camp. Six miles has never seemed so long. The wind is brutal. We fight to set up our tents. I try to look at the thermometer/compass attached to my jacket and flailing in the wind. 20 degrees Fahrenheit, 35 mph winds equals 20 degrees BELOW ZERO wind chill factor, it says. It certainly feels like it. We finally secure the tent, tying each pole to a 25-pound rock and hoping the tent can handle the stress. I hear those words of the backpacker heading down the mountain several hours earlier: "Several parties' tents were destroyed during the night from the high winds… they had to descend to Outpost Camp (at 10,360 feet) to make it through the night…" I'm hoping we won't be the next victims of the storm.

We had heard over and over again, in the weeks prior to our trek: "No one can predict what happens to the body at over 12,000 feet." My headache won't go away, and my stomach doesn't feel great. Tim's cough hasn't stopped since we hit 8,400 feet. Tim begins to notice his fingers and toes are tingling. Shawn's extremities feel numb.

A solo hiker stumbles past through the camp. He looks like a drunk leaving a bar at 4:00 am. With slurred speech, he tells us he was completely lost for 3 hours. He finally found the original trail and made the decision to descend. Each of us, without saying a word, knows that this could be us. That guy is lucky to still be alive. In his state, the trail's precipitous 2000-foot drop-offs are a blink-of-an-eye away. We feared he could easily step off the trail and plummet to his death.

Thursday, September 18, 1997, 8:00 pm:

Night falls. We know the next several hours are critical to our success or failure. The wind howls through the night. It beats and pushes the tent, testing every seam as well as the guy-lines securing the tent to the mountain. We know that a good night's rest is essential. We're all exhausted, our bodies demanding what the elevation refuses to provide: oxygen. In a resting state, our breathing is much shallower. However, the only way to get the oxygen to our organs, at this altitude, is to breathe deeply. That dichotomy means a good night's sleep is a rare thing up here. Before crashing, Shawn says, "If it's as bad tomorrow as it is today, it's probably wise to head down the mountain…" We all agree, but no one says a word.

At midnight, I awake. The wind is still whipping. I notice something strange outside: There's light. The clouds didn't stand up to the wind as well as our tents have: they're gone, replaced by a million stars and a moon that lights up the landscape like the sun's own rays. My only thought is that we'll actually have a chance tomorrow for the summit. I close my eyes again. Surprisingly, my headache and stomachache have gone away. I know that acclimating at 12,000 feet means our chance for success at 14,500 feet is even greater.

Friday, September 19, 1997, 3:00 am:

Again, I'm awakened by the wind. But it's not the brutal wind that tortured us hours before; it's a gentle wind that's keeping our window of opportunity open, forcing the storm clouds out to the Pacific Ocean where they started. I know that now is the time to make an attempt at the ascent. I wake Shawn and Tim and we all agreed that this opportunity won't last forever.

We struggle to get the stove lit. The wind and oxygen-deprived air are two ingredients for a cold meal. Bringing the stove inside the tent turns out to be the only way Shawn can boil water for his dehydrated meal. But I can't wait – before the water even comes to a boil, I consume my MRE and a couple energy bars. Amazingly, I'm still hungry. At this elevation, the body requires 5000-6000 calories per day – twice that of the sea-level recommended daily allowance. *(Note: if circumstances require you to bring your stove into the tent to boil water, ensure you vent the tent so that you have airflow to ensure that you have sufficient oxygen to breathe (and let carbon monoxide out), and also be sure the flame is contained – synthetic tents will melt/catch on fire).*

With the wind and warmth from the sun, the temperature is easily -35 degrees Fahrenheit. We throw on every single layer of clothing we brought with us. We look like the stereotypical kid in a snowsuit, with layers upon layers underneath, who can't put his arms at his side. While I feel comfortable, Tim and Shawn are shivering. Tim wraps his sleeping bag around his torso and will use that as his parka for the rest of the trek.

I begin organizing and packing my day pack. This pack will need to contain all the essentials to reach the summit in any condition – my hydration pack, a water bottle, water filter/purifier, an MRE, several energy bars, energy shots, Gatorade orange mix, and a handful of sugar packets (at this elevation, the body has a difficult time digesting fats and proteins due to the lack of oxygen reaching the stomach; straight simple carbohydrates are required to fuel the body), headlamp, mini-flashlight, extra lithium batteries, emergency (space) blanket, cellular phone, lighter, whistle, Swiss Army knife, compass, map, first aid kit, disposable panoramic camera, sunscreen and sunglasses. I have no clothing to bring; I'm wearing it all. The only items left behind are the tent, sleeping bag, and the remaining food, which we hung off a rock overhang to keep the marmots and bears from getting it.

At 5:15 am we start hiking in the dark to Trail Camp Lake. We're out of water and this is the last water source on the trail. We pass a party of three who are huddled together, fighting hypothermia. Each has an emergency blanket and is counting the minutes until the sun rises. They're shaking pretty badly and don't look too good, but apparently have their minds set to climb the summit.

When we arrive at the lake, a quarter mile up from our base camp, we don't expect what we're seeing. The lake had begun to freeze overnight. I climb out on a rock to find a gap in the ice and try pumping the first of our water bottles. The process is very slow. It's hard to grip the bottle in this bone-chilling cold, and it suddenly slips from my hands. I react quickly to save the water bottle, a critical inventory item, from being lost in the black lake. This little slip causes a large amount of water to splash on my pants and gloves, which makes me panic for a second – soaking wet gloves and pants in these extreme conditions could be a nightmare. But to my pleasant surprise, the water, when it hits, instantly freezes! I brush off the newly-formed ice crystals and continue pumping icy water into my bottle, hoping the filter would continue to work. These lakes are prime candidates for

Giardia and other bacteria that could ruin your intestinal tracks, or worse.

The sun begins to creep over the horizon. The 14,000-foot range of peaks above the lake is painted a color gold that our eyes will never forget. Stunning Alpenglow. We drop everything in awe. The peaks have changed from black, to gray, to gold, and when the sun rises, they fade to their natural tan in a matter of minutes. Only the sun's pure light hits these peaks up here; there's no polluted atmosphere to get in the way.

Friday, September 19, 1997, 6:00 am:

We begin our ascent. Five miles of steep trail climbing 2500 vertical feet awaits us. It is called the 97-Switchbacks. The path is cut into the granite walls, winding up the mountain, back and forth 97 times to allow trekkers a little bit of a break as they literally climb straight up. Shawn's altimeter watch is our guide and our governor. We agree to stop every 250 vertical feet, rest for a couple minutes, then resume the climb. We do not know how our bodies will react as we exert ourselves at this altitude and believe that if we allow our bodies to adjust, the summit will be a step closer to being ours.

Our pace is steady but not overly aggressive. Quickly we gain elevation and can see the valley widen below us. Massive mountains and lakes become hills and ponds from our vantage point. I am beginning to get really warm now. I peel off the wool hat, Gore-Tex gloves, waterproof pants, and the mid-weight thermal top. The air is crisp, and the sun is strong up here; the sunglasses and sunscreen are essential. It is a perfect day. We're blessed with ideal weather and hiking conditions. We celebrate when we reach 13,000 feet – a new milestone!

The views are magnificent, but the path is narrow and rocky and one wrong step means certain death. Shawn tells me he feels dizzy, and there's some sort of liquid sloshing around in his lungs. Tim's cough persists. My headache throbs with each step. When my stomach doesn't feel great, I eat more energy bars and drink more water. Shawn's altimeter watch, like many altimeter watches, decides it's too high for it to function, and stops. We maxed it out! We know it's above 13,000 and know it's less than 14,500 feet. At this time, we each feel good enough to continue, and do.

Trail Crest sits at 13,777 feet. We have traversed the 3 miles of trail that makes up the 97-Switchbacks. We rest for a brief time. I now wish I'd left some of those layers on. Trail Crest is a mountain saddle: A high mountain pass where the wind is gusting from all sides and there's nothing to provide protection from it. On one side is the valley we came from and know intimately; on the other is beautiful, pristine wilderness, snowcapped mountains, and huge lakes. The view is amazing. The next hundred yards of trail is the John Muir trail. It descends some until we see a fork in the trail and sign that says MOUNT WHITNEY – 2 MILES.

Those two miles are absolutely brutal. My muscles are getting tired, and the wind and altitude bear down on me. My small daypack seems to weigh a ton. My muscles are getting tired and the wind and altitude bear down on me. I begin to wish I'd spent more time on the Stairmaster and treadmill. I take fifty steps and rest. Take fifty more, and rest. 50, rest. 50, rest. 50, rest. Shawn and Tim are ahead of me, and the gap widens. While teamwork has gotten us this far, it is clearly our individual strength and willpower that is the determinant of our personal successes now. A thousand thoughts race through my mind. I think of my wife, my family, my friends. I thank God for the strength to take these challenging steps. I feel blessed to breathe in this crisp mountain air and the indescribable beauty around me. The top looks close enough that it tempts me to continue, but far enough away to cause me to question myself with each step. 50, rest. 50, rest. 50, rest. 25, rest. 25, rest. 25, rest.

Friday, September 19, 1997, 11:30 am:

I look up and am shocked to realize I'm a stone's throw away from the summit. Adrenaline takes over. My headache is gone, my stomach feels great, my legs feel strong. Everything is perfect. I quicken my pace. When I see the stone shelter built in 1909 by the Smithsonian Institution, I know I've done it. 200 yards, 100 yards, 50 yards, 25 yards, 10, 5, 1... I am there!!!

I let out a yell: "YEAHHHHHHHHH – TOP OF THE WORLD!!!!!!!!!" There is a register at the top. I sign in and under Comments, I simply write "AWESOME!"

There were so many obstacles for us to reach this point, and so many people who didn't think we would make it to the top. But we did. Individually, we celebrate our success. Then, we celebrate together. We share the incredible views, and we share the satisfaction of knowing that we are at the top of the continental United States. On August 18, 1873, Mount Whitney was climbed for the first time in history. And September 19, 1997, one hundred twenty-four years later, three friends overcame many challenges and climbed the tallest Mountain in the Lower 48. A day we will never forget.

We eat at the top and savor the view and the meal as though it were our first and our last. The journey down the mountain is rapid. Elevation during a descent is your friend. The air seems to thicken with each step we take. As we're heading down the mountain, and tired and altitude-sick climbers are heading up. "Almost there…" we'd say in encouragement. "Don't give up, it's worth it!"

Trail camp at 12,000 feet is a sight for sore eyes. However, dreams of pizza and a warm bed are more enticing. We quickly pack up our gear and continue the hike down the mountain. Our legs are exhausted, our lungs overworked. Darkness won't wait for us; we hike in the dark. Seeing the lights from cars at the trailhead, we know we're almost home.

Friday, September 19, 1997, 8:30 pm:

We've hiked continuously for over 15 hours, traversing 16 miles of terrain, a total of twenty-two miles since we left this very spot 33 hours ago. What a trip, what an adventure!

"So", I asked, "which mountain do you want to climb next?!..."

We decide our next climb will be another formidable mountain in California: Mount Shasta, which towers at 14,180 feet around 500 miles North of here. It will be our first mountaineering experience with ice axes, crampons, and being roped together on our way to the summit.

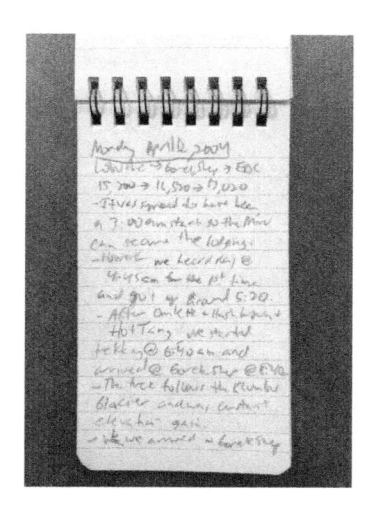

APPENDIX B:
MOUNT EVEREST BASE CAMP (2004)

Friday, April 2, 2004
Altitude: Sea Level
Singapore:

I wake up @ 5:30 am, all packed and ready to go! It's very hard to say "Bye" to Ivett and the kids. When I'm on a business trip, I know I'll get to call each night and say "Hi" and "I love you and I miss you" to the family. But unfortunately, there's no mobile phone infrastructure where we'll be in the Himalayas — we'll be completely off the grid.

I'm still feeling the after-effects of the 3rd rabies vaccination I had on March 30th. High fever and still slightly dizzy — this is the worst I've felt in a long time. But the rabies vaccination is essential in Nepal — loose and rabid dogs populate Kathmandu and the high country, and it's better to feel sick due to the vaccination vs. feeling sick at 13,000 feet with no medical facilities around.

Chris hired a taxi from the Singapore Four Seasons Hotel and is at our apartment at 5:50 am. Traffic is light, and we make it to Changi Airport with plenty of time to spare.

Our Thai Airways flight from Singapore to Bangkok is uneventful. Before boarding, Chris offers me the window seat, so I can observe the majestic Himalayas from 39,000 feet. What a true gentleman!

When we get on the plane, much to our dismay, there's a big solid wall area which will serve as my "window" for the flight! It isn't actually that bad when I recline the seat. Hitting Nepal's airspace is a bit anti-climactic — it's very overcast, and we can see just a piece of a large mountain peeking briefly through the clouds.

Next is airport security, immigration, and customs. Ahh – we should have taken care of visas in advance! Two long hours later, we finally finish that process. I'm still battling a recurring fever from the rabies vaccine, this time in the form of cold sweats as we go through immigration. (I feel like George Costanza, sweating profusely for no reason!)

We find our driver, and after 15 minutes of trying – and failing – to start the engine, Chris hops out to push the car. Eventually, the clutch-popping approach works, and we're off to Kathmandu city.

We arrive at the Kathmandu Guest House, an establishment which has a history all its own. It's one of the longest-standing hotels in this part of the city and has hosted many celebrity guests. Our room overlooks the restaurant and courtyard.

We wander around the vicinity of the hotel, checking out the many shops – mountaineering stores, restaurants, "hippy hangouts" as they're called here, etc. It's a bit surprising to be offered pot, but I guess that's why many dig this city. We haggle for souvenir shirts, patches, and prayer flags.

For dinner we go to the Rum Doodle restaurant, another legendary establishment. It's named after an old British book about 4 blokes and a 40,000½-foot peak.

It's amazing to see the Yeti-sized wooden feet mementoes/plaques signed by many Everest climbers from expeditions over the years, covering every wall and ceiling of the establishment. Seeing a wooden foot signed by Sir Edmond Hillary is absolutely awesome and really puts the trip into perspective. The waiter gives us a wooden foot for us to write our own inspirational message. Chris has a great idea – we'll carry it up the mountain and hang it at one of the high-altitude mountain huts!

There's no indoor seating available tonight, as the place is packed with trekkers and climbers, so we're sitting outdoors under the canopy while the rain pours down and the wind howls. My fever has kicked into high gear, and all I can think about is getting some sleep and kicking this fever once and for all.

Saturday, April 3, 2004
Altitude: 4,300 feet
Kathmandu:

We meet Naresh, part of the Spirit Adventures team, along with the tour guide for our day in Kathmandu city. Due to yesterday's violent clash between the government and demonstrators, there's a "strike" today – in Nepali terms, that means "no motor vehicles permitted". Tires are burning in all intersections across the city to warn drivers to stay away. Apparently, protesters throw rocks at any cars driving "illegally."

We walk from the Kathmandu Guest House all around town passing many stray dogs. Chris, who didn't get the rabies vaccination, is a bit more paranoid than I am – especially after being charged by a big, mean dog yesterday!

I do what the Nepalis do: walk very, very slowly past the dogs and through town. The slow pace is good due to the fever that won't subside, and as a result I'm definitely not overdoing it.

We see a very impressive Tibetan Buddhist temple known as "Monkey Temple," and I spin all the prayer wheels as I walk around the grounds. When spinning Buddhist prayer wheels, you must only use your right hand, and walk around the building clockwise as you spin. The Buddhists believe that when you spin the wheels, the prayers inscribed on the wheels are released up to the heavens. Juniper bows are being burned nearby. They give off a unique scent; it's a bit pungent but very pleasant.

Despite the temple's name, there are only a few monkeys to be seen. Our guide explains these are the only survivors of the monkey flu which wiped out a large number of the inhabitants the prior year.

At a souvenir stand next to the temple, I see a beautifully carved piece of slate inscribed with "Om Mani Padme Hum" in Tibetan Sanskrit. Our guide translates my conversation with the vendor. The guide explains that the slate was created by a "new" artist, who turns out to be a tough negotiator! I pay more than I had budgeted, but it was an amazing piece, and worth every penny. To make me feel good about the negotiation, the artist throws in a sun/moon necklace for free! He tells us this is his very first sale (which makes it a very special/auspicious occasion), and he starts to give thanks to his God.

We walk through the old part of town. It's pretty enlightening to see how people live outside the hustle and bustle of the city center. It appears to be a very poor area with tough conditions — although not as poor as some of the homes I saw during my visit to rural India.

We then arrive at Durbar Square, where, apparently, violence broke out yesterday. We had been warned by our guide that we may not be able to go there if there were any tensions in the air. We quickly agreed!

The Square backs onto the Palace and some old temples and structures. The "commercial" holy men with painted faces and dreadlocks attempt to get their photos taken for money. We're told that the "living Goddess" glances out the window of her palace once a day. (Sadly, it happened earlier in the day and we didn't catch a glimpse.) The Square also connects with a road called "Freak Street" - the guide explains that it's named this for apparently obvious reasons. We collectively decide not to explore.

We then meet up with the owner of the local guide company as well as our guide for the trek. We eat a late lunch while talking about their lives in Nepal, and life in general. It's great meeting them and hearing their perspectives!

As soon as the meal ends, we head back to the hotel to drop off our stuff. Still fighting the fever, I fall asleep, waking up in time for a quick dinner and packing, after which I go straight back to bed. The rest is much needed, and we haven't even set foot on the mountain yet!

Sunday April 4, 2004
Altitude: 4,300 feet –> 9,300 feet –> 8,450 feet
Kathmandu to Lukla to Phakding:

I wake up early again due to the normal daily ruckus coming from the courtyard adjacent to our room. I jump into the shower, and let me tell you, there's nothing like encountering two 4-inch-long leeches climbing the shower wall at head level to start your day! I have one of the fast showers on record, praying that the leeches won't leap out and get me! We couldn't be more excited to be checking out of the hotel today and getting into the mountains.

Vehicles are permitted to run this morning, which is a relief as we need to get to the airport to fly to Lukla. So, after 30 minutes of trying to track down copier paper to make a copy of the required travel insurance policy to provide to the guide company, we make our way to the airport. Good thing we allotted buffer time this morning – despite the delay, we make it to the airport with time to spare.

After a few minor delays, our flight finally takes off. It's a very old plane, apparently weighing only 7282 pounds, which is very light for an aircraft. We're flying from Kathmandu to Lukla, a STOL (Short Take Off and Landing) airstrip at 9,300-foot elevation. The air is very thin at this elevation, and the landing strip is literally on the side of the mountain, which is why the plane is light and baggage is limited.

Our guide Raj tells us the left side of the plane has the best views of the big mountains, and fortunately, we manage to get the last two seats on the left. It's very hazy and cloudy, and the scratched old windows aren't helping – we don't see much at first. Suddenly, Chris sees the mountains pierce through the clouds – how amazing! We're completely in awe as we get our first glimpse of the Himalayas.

I glance down at my altimeter watch, which was reading over 9000 feet, and realize we're about to land. We look straight ahead, peering out the pilot's windshield of this tiny plane, and it seems as though we're going to crash into the side of the mountain!

In fact, the airport at Lukla is notorious for being one of the most dangerous in the world. The runway is extremely short and angles up the mountain to slow the plane down to land. There are a few white knuckles on board as we grab anything we can, to brace ourselves for the landing. We land without incident, and the small group of trekkers in the cabin applaud.

We walk to a restaurant for breakfast, already breathing quite heavily due to the altitude. There's a table set up near the entrance to the restaurant, and we're asked to participate in a Diamox/Gingko study on altitude sickness being conducted by University of Chicago research students. I listened to the students describe the project, but ultimately declined – while I had Diamox with me, my intent was to climb without ingesting it to see if and how I would acclimatize naturally.

As we're eating, we learn that a very important Lama (even more important than the Dalai Lama, we are told) will be coming to Lukla shortly. Talking about an auspicious beginning to our trek! We wait and wait – "shortly" turns into a couple hours - but we're excited about the opportunity to see this Lama! Then with the sound of loud Tibetan Long Horns and the smell of juniper burning, we see the Lama being carried into the area nearby. What a very special experience – especially watching the local population's reactions. This was well worth the wait! Now we're really ready to start the trek.

Despite the elevation, I'm finally feeling back to normal since I became sick with bronchitis almost two weeks ago. And, today the fever from that 3rd rabies shot is finally behind me as well.

Looking around at the scenery, the mountains, the valley, the rivers, and especially the people, it suddenly hits me: "Wow, I am trekking in Nepal!" I'm so amazed at all the porters from various trekking parties who have converged at this high-altitude starting point. It looks like they are carrying 100 pounds in a rudimentary pack/bag, strapped to their heads, while wearing sandals! Hard, hard labor, and strong people. (*Note: Westerners typically refer to them as "Sherpas"; however, Sherpa is a specific term referring to an ethnic group in eastern Nepal.*)

We quickly notice how warm and friendly the locals are, including the little kids we see who say "NAMASTE!" (meaning "Hello/goodbye" in Nepalese) in their tiny voices. I begin saying it constantly – it's amazing how good it feels sharing that basic greeting with the locals as well as the other trekkers – I can't help but smile and be happy.

When we arrive at the Namaste Lodge in Phakding, which is at 8,450 feet elevation, I feel strong. Fortunately, we make it inside just before the rains begin.

To minimize the weight being carried and maximize the experience, we chose to stay at "tea houses" for the entire trek in the mountains. They are spread up and down the mountain, offering tea, boiled water, food, warmth, and lodging for trekkers traversing this section of the Himalayas.

Monday April 5, 2004
Altitude: 8,450 feet –> 11,110 feet
Phakding to Namche Bazaar:

We begin the trek from Phakding at 8:30 am. It will be the toughest of the "low-altitude" trek days as we expect to climb nearly 3000 feet in 5 or so hours. The guidebooks warn that many trekkers go up this section of the trek too quickly and get altitude sickness. Fortunately, that won't be a problem for me today – the altitude is pushing my lungs and I take it slow. I do feel rushed a few times trying to keep up with our team who are pushing a brisk pace, or being rushed by the masses of porters and/or "yamoos" (*the term used by our guide for the half-yak/half-cows that inhabit the lower altitudes of the Himalayas, officially called a dzo*). At that moment I ask myself, "Are these Beasts of Burden or Ships of the Mountains?!" It's incredible, the difficult work that the porters and the dzo/yak do to help the westerners get up the mountain. It's also challenging dodging the dzo/yak dung on the trails, but that's part of the deal.

About halfway to Namche Bazaar, our destination for the night, we stop by a small village called Monjo at 9,300 feet for lunch. I must say that it's the best spaghetti and tomato sauce with onions I've ever had. The onions are so flavorful in the Himalayas – it's hard to describe the taste!

At about 10,500 feet, we're stopped by what appear to be seven soldiers with machine guns on the trail. We don't know whether they're Nepali military or Maoist rebels. (*The latter have been in a violent clash to overthrow the Nepali government for the past few years and have recently been robbing tourist trekkers*). They're quizzing Raj as he fumbles around with his pack, trying to find some paperwork. The soldiers search his pack, and Chris and I wonder if this is the end of the trek… or worse. Before long, the soldiers send us on our way. They are indeed Nepali Army (the good guys), and they were just making sure we aren't bomb-carrying Maoists. It's all a little unnerving, as you can imagine, but better the heightened security than being the victim of a high-altitude bombing attack!

After this delay, we trek with purpose all the way up to 11,110 feet, towards the top of Namche Bazaar, the Sherpa capital and well-stocked outpost sitting at over two vertical miles in the air. We'll be staying at the Tashi Delek Lodge tonight. Raj says the place is really nice and that they have an IMAX theater! I'm shocked and excited at the thought of a high-altitude IMAX theater! Needless to say, there is no theater; something has definitely been lost in translation there! That said, this will be the nicest tea house/lodge we stay in. Hot showers and everything! Chris is pretty beat, and while he rests, I go shopping around Namche. I bump into Jerry, a French trekker who we saw in Lukla and Phakding. The two of us stop at a quaint German bakery where I have some incredible apple crumb cake and hot milk tea. I'm not much of a tea drinker, but after having hot tea with milk and sugar, I'm a convert!

When I get back to the lodge, I wait for a couple of hours to use the shower due to the massive queue. In the meantime, we order Mixed Noodles – kind of like Lo Mein – it is excellent! This becomes our go-to meal while at this lodge.

In the morning, my breakfast of choice is an egg omelet with onions. The onions in Monjo yesterday blew my mind, and with eggs today, made the most extraordinary breakfast!

A few things that happen in the dining area of the lodge keep us laughing all week:

First, there's a trekker, part of a very large trekking group, who just does not stop playing his harmonica! He's driving us nuts! We name him "Wally The Harmonicist" as we try to tune him out.

Next, the Sherpa woman who owns the place has a newborn baby. Besides giving quite a show breastfeeding in front of everyone gathered in the busy dining area, she changes her baby's diaper and puts the dirty cloth diaper on one of the diner tables where tourists are eating. As if dining with the aroma of a rotten diaper invading our nasal passages during dinner wasn't enough, she then uses the dirty diaper to wipe off one of the tables! It was very funny watching this unfold, but also very scary. The next morning, as we arrive for breakfast, they offer to seat us at that table. I politely say, "no thank you - we prefer to sit next to the window with the view of the snow-capped mountains"!

When I return to the room after a post-breakfast shower, Chris informs me that I missed another show: one of the old women trekkers flashed her boobs in the dining room!

Lastly, a stray male horse walks by the lodge early one afternoon. All of a sudden, we hear loud squealing and grunting noises, and see the horse attempt to mount the owner's mare. The male bites the female, prompting the owner's kids to throw rocks at him. I've never seen a horse run so fast!

I'm sure these anecdotes don't sound funny at all, but when you're at 11,000 feet, breathing in thin air, seeing all this silly stuff play out like a Monty Python skit, it's hard not to be laughing your butt off!

Tuesday April 6, 2004
Altitude: 11,110 feet –> 12,370 feet –> 11,110 feet
Namche Bazaar to Everest View and Back:

Notes from the day:

- Acclimatization Day
- Snow at night
- First glimpse of Everest, Ama Dablam, and Lhotse peaks
- Tsering Gyaltsen (Tenzing Norgay's grandson): We had learned before leaving Singapore/Sydney that our employer had done a volunteer project with Tsering to put internet on Base Camp a couple years earlier. We were able to arrange for a meeting with Tsering, which was extremely exciting, especially when we learned that he was the grandson of Tenzing Norgay, the first Sherpa to summit Mount Everest with Sir Edmund Hillary back in 1953. When we meet with Tsering, he shows us maps and models of Khumbu and the Base Camp, describing how the solution was implemented. He shares that because the Khumbu Glacier is always moving down the valley, the team had to adjust the satellites around Base Camp every few days to ensure it picked up the signal, so the people temporarily living/staying at Everest Base Camp could stay connected.
- # of Rescue Helicopters
- Meru's (porter) day off
- Run across to ridge (Chris and I)
- Monastery

- Khumbu 3D Model
- Room with a view – bed and bath
- Yak trails
- Discuss the proper order when using a baby wipe to clean your body!
- Last antibiotic pill! I was finally finished with the antibiotics that I started in Singapore to combat the bronchitis!
- Chris and his Gingko from the Med Student study 125 gingko 125 diamox
- Snow
- Khumjung Village/School, aka the Hillary School, founded by Sir Edmund Hillary in 1961 to give back to the Everest region. After learning about the project with Tsering to get internet at base camp, and now learning about the Sir Edmund Hillary's school at Khumjung, I feel remiss in not doing some sort of charitable event while being blessed to have seen and experienced such an amazing country, region, culture and people.

Wednesday April 7, 2004
Altitude: 11,110 feet –> 12,620 feet
Namche Bazaar to Pangboche/Everest View Lodge:

Notes from the day:
- Snow

- Breakfast with Tsering
- Tengboche Monastery
- Long day of trekking due no lodges/tea huts available in Tengboche
- High Lama in helicopter – dropped rice to bless the people – I pick up 1 grain of rice (put in camera case – I wonder where that is now?)
- After Tengboche, the crowds thin significantly
- Glad we push to Pangboche to accelerate the trek a bit
- 1 Extra Day created – we determined as we mapped out the remaining days

Thursday April 8, 2004
Altitude: 12,610 feet –> 13,920 feet
Pangboche to Dingboche:

On this day, the concept of this book is born. In my notes I call it: 5 Elements of Trekking Success:

- ❖ Mental/Spiritual Strength and Endurance
- ❖ Physical Strength and Endurance
- ❖ Altitude Strength and Endurance
- ❖ Iron Constitution (Fight Disease)
- ❖ Strong Family Support
- ❖ Chris offered up "Gore-Tex" as the 6th element of success – thin air at play, yet he's absolutely right how critical it is.

- Our porter Meru is a bit slower today
- Chris mentioned that our guide Raj is a bit cranky today – it's the altitude
- Leave at 8:15 am, arrive at lodge at 10:55 am
- Try making 2 Sat (satellite) phone calls to the family at home – leave 2 messages.
- Take a nap in the sun – much needed rest and relaxation
- Morning – most incredible mountain landscapes I've ever seen!
- Hotel = Peak 38 View Lodge, with incredible views of Ama Dablam, Island Peak, Thamserku, Lhotse, Lhotse Shar
- Light lunch (vegetable noodle soup) – much needed carb break after multiple days of fried mixed veggies and noodles
- Everyone is a little quieter today - more inward focus given the high altitude we are now trekking in
- Last night was the highest elevation I've ever slept at – and I slept great
- Even at this altitude (13,900 feet), I've acclimatized well, and it feels like 9,000 feet
- No headache, no stomachache, etc. - just thin air which I'm breathing heavily to consume!

Raj seems to have taken us to the highest lodge in the highest part of the village — we did that in Namche, Pangboche, and after no vacancy in the first few lodges in Dingboche, Chris and I (apparently o Raj's dismay) push for the highest lodge again!! We feel it's a good strategy to get a couple hundred extra more vertical feet elevation for sleep (to aid acclimatization) and also, in the morning, we've been able to skip the congestion of trekkers in the village.

Overall Timeline at this stage of the trek:

4/2/04 - Singapore to Kathmandu
4/3/04 - Kathmandu
4/4/04 - Kathmandu to Lukla to Phakding
4/5/04 - Phakding to Namche Bazaar
4/6/04 - Namche Bazaar
4/7/04 - Namche Bazaar to Pangboche
4/8/04 - Pangboche to Dingboche
4/9/04 - Dingboche to Chukhung
4/10/04 - Chukhung to Chukhung Ri via Kongma-La
4/11/04 - Chukhung to Lobuche
4/12/04 - Lobuche to Gorak Shep (Kala Patthar?)
4/13/04 - Gorak Shep to Mount Everest Base Camp (EBC)
4/14/04 - Gorak Shep to Pumori Base Camp to Pangboche
4/15/04 - Pangboche to Namche Bazaar
4/16/04 - Namche Bazaar to Thami (Tsering)
4/17/04 - Namche Bazaar to Lukla
4/18/04 - Lukla to Kathmandu (in the morning), with a Kathmandu Tour in the afternoon
4/19/04 - Kathmandu to Singapore

Glancing out of the window at 5:39 pm, I realize the beautiful deep blue skies and white snow-covered mountains have transformed to a cold gray. I think to myself, "To win this mental game, we need to see the Blue and White through all of the Gray!"

Friday April 9, 2004
Altitude: 13,920 feet –> 15,180 feet
Dingboche to Chukhung:

Notes from the day:

- We leave the tea house at ~8:30 am and arrive at Chukhung at ~10:30 am.
- Today the mountains are the most spectacular we've seen: Ama Dablam, Lhotse, Lhotse Shar – they just keep getting bigger, closer and more impressive with each step we take.
- Chris and I agree to take the walk to Chukhung slowly.
- Chris has a throbbing headache.
- I'm still feeling strong (but definitely need more sleep!)
- I am now at the highest altitude I've ever been.
- It's also the strongest I've felt at altitude – it's amazing when you acclimatize properly, how good you can feel even at this altitude.
- We're at 15,000+ feet – we'll stay here overnight and then attempt Chukhung Ri @ 5550 meters or ~18,200 feet tomorrow – this will be nearly as tall as Kala Patthar.
- Then we'll return to and sleep at Chukhung @ ~15,200 feet.

- It's a bit risky, but if the "Climb high, sleep low" mantra works, we should feel quite strong
- We'll then push over Kongma-La mountain pass the following day and sleep at about 16,000 feet at Lobuche.
- The next two nights will be at Gorak Shep (17,200 feet)
- Again, if the climb-high-sleep-low mantra works, we should be really strong for Everest Base Camp and Pumori Base Camp
- I'll let you know tomorrow night how we feel!

Saturday April 10, 2004
Altitude: 15,180 feet –> 18,198 feet –> 15, 180 feet
Chukhung to Chukhung Ri and Return:

Another rest day, this time with a great day hike and a summit of Chukhung Ri peak, to push our acclimatization. We leave at 8:00 am for the day hike and return at about 12:45 pm.

Definitely the most incredible mountain landscapes as of yet – Ama Dablam, Pumori, Makalu, Lhotse, Lhotse Shar, Nuptse, plus the Nuptse Glacier

The ascent is 2000 vertical feet in ~2 hours – a very fast ascent in my book, especially at this altitude!

Sunday April 11, 2004
Altitude: 15,180 feet –> 18,100 feet –> 15,700 feet
Chukhung to Kongma-La to Lobuche:

We see this makeshift route over Kongma-La pass as an opportunity to shave a day (and the resulting wear and tear) off our approach to Everest Base Camp by taking this rarely used high pass. It also affords us another opportunity to climb high and sleep low; a plan that has played out well for us over the past few days at high elevation. Fortunately, with a great guide company and great guide and porter, we're able to modify the trek on the fly.

- We start out at 7:00 am, arrive at 2:30 pm.
- Tough trek over this high pass.
- We see a tahr, a species of Himalayan deer, at nearly 17,000 feet. Incredible seeing wildlife at this altitude.

This trail is not visibly marked or heavily worn like everywhere else this trek. There's definitely bush-whacking and trail-blazing to make our way up and over this pass. We are above the tree line at this stage so we carefully assess which way we should turn to make our way back to the main trail route safely. Periodically we hear rocks falling from above, and debris go flying by. Now I can see why this isn't a formal trail with the potential rockslide danger. We really have to watch our steps today.

Strenuous, but no tourists and no yaks to contend with! While it's great to meet like-minded adventurers trekking to a common destination, at altitude I find that I'd rather be where it's a bit more remote so that we're not dealing with tourist's loud chatter late into the night or early morning disturbing our precious sleep. Also, tons of tourists lead to tons of congestion on the trails/tea houses, making everything slow and negatively impacting progress to the daily arrival goals.

As for the yaks, they're incredible animals which have somehow adapted to a world with very thin air. They're also absolutely critical to enable climbers to make it to their destination, and also enable the tea houses to stock their business so they can make a living as well. That said, aside from dodging endless yak dung for miles and miles on the trail, it's a bit nerve-racking as you're passing the yaks trekking to your destination for the day. The trails are often very narrow and just barely etched into the walls in the mountain; sometimes they're just wide enough for you to pass, with a 1000-foot drop if you make a mistake. It seems like at every tight spot on the trail there are a group of yaks, loaded with the gear they are carrying up the mountain, trying to squeeze by on that same bit of narrow trail. I can't count how many times I thought I would get bumped into and either drop 1000 feet to my untimely death or get crushed against the wall on the other side of the narrow trail. Also, there are many long, rickety suspension bridges crossing large valleys and rivers along the trek. Even if another trekker or two are walking on the bridge, the thing is bouncing around and creaking from the strain. Add the normal winds whipping down these valleys and it's a white knuckler! Then, inevitably, when you're halfway across, somehow there's a fully loaded yak heading right towards you. In cases like this, there's no mountain wall to be smashed against – it's a 1000-foot drop on either side, into a rocky and icy racing Himalayan river born from the snow melt of these massive peaks watching overhead. You must hang on for dear life as they pass!

And now you know the reason for my delight to traversing a pass with no tourists and no yaks!

Monday April 12, 2004
Altitude: 15,700 feet –> 16,520 feet –> 17,600 feet –> 16,520 feet
Lobuche to Gorak Shep to Everest Base Camp (EBC) back to Gorak Shep:

Today was supposed to be an early start. Last night we agreed that we'd have a 3:00 am start so that our porter could secure the lodging at this busy lodge. At 4:45 am we're briefly awakened by Raj's voice, but fall back to sleep due to exhaustion, only waking back up at 5:20 am. No one complains, as we really need the extra sleep. We just keep our fingers crossed that we'll be able to lock in a place to sleep for the night.

Half of me is a little frustrated that each day we are searching for lodging and that it wasn't locked in before we even stepped foot on the mountain. We risk not having a place to stay, which is what happened to Tengboche a couple days earlier. We did not have tents – only sleeping bags – so, while we could have bivouacked in an emergency (albeit illegally), but it would have been risky, as at any moment a storm could've blown in and dumped snow and heavy winds on us. In every other major trek that I've done, precise logistics are essential, and reservations for permits, campsites, lodging, etc. had to be done months in advance. We were nervous, especially during the current Himalayan high season, that we might be left out in the cold.

That said, the other half of me likes how we we're able to customize the trek on the fly. We cut out that Tengboche day and decided to do the Chukhung Ri pass route and cut out another day.

We couldn't have done this if the lodging/routing had been set in stone. It's a balance, and so far we've been lucky.

After a tasty omelet, hash browns, and hot Tang breakfast, we start trekking at 6:40 am. This portion of the trek follows the massive Khumbu Glacier and is constant elevation gain as we climb this morning.

When we arrive at Gorak Shep's tea house at 8:40 am, we get some food prepared for our lunch on the trail: fried veg momos, potatoes, a cinnamon bun, and chapati with peanut butter. Needless to say, the alpine cinnamon bun and peanut butter do not make it out of the lodge, it's so delicious!

The trek to Everest Base Camp is long, hard, and absolutely incredible, from the massive glacier itself, to the stunning views of Nuptse, to the legendary Khumbu Icefall in the distance, to the downed helicopter lying lifeless at 17,000 feet after crashing a couple years earlier, to the first glimpses of the Base Camp and Everest itself, showing itself from behind other tall neighboring mountains along the way.

When we reach Everest Base Camp (EBC), Meru, our porter, goes to work; we really want to meet some of the climbing teams whose adventure starts where ours would leave off. He sees one of his friends and is able to get us an invitation to the Chilean Expedition's Base Camp! Amazing!

Nimba Sherpa is the Base Camp leader, and we meet one of the Chilean climbers and photographers.

We're told that Nimba Sherpa was the Base Camp leader for Chris Bonington's Everest expeditions. We're also told that two climbers from Singapore are traversing the Khumbu Icefall and heading up to Advanced Base Camp to acclimatize with the Chilean and Sherpa climbers. That's really cool, as I've been living in Singapore the past couple of years. Who would have known we'd be on the mountain at the same time! (*Note that about a month after we see the Chilean team, we learn that four of them summited Mount Everest.*)

On the way back from EBC, it starts to snow, and continues to accumulate as we head back to Gorak Shep lodge.

Interesting night tonight. There's a group of trekkers that arrive in the dining area about the same time we do. They're a lively bunch and appear to be enjoying the multiple rounds of Nepalese beer. As the Sherpa people revere the mountains as sacred, I do not drink alcohol while on the mountain (I also know it will interfere with acclimatization, which is another compelling reason to abstain for the few days we're in the mountains). This group is brave enough to order the yak stew for dinner. At the start of the trek, I stuck to a predominately vegetarian and eggs diet and avoided meat for two reasons: the locals are primarily vegetarian, and more importantly during the trek, we'd see Sherpa porters heading up to the lodges with slabs of yak meat strapped to their backs for the tourist trekkers. The meat is completely unrefrigerated and spends hours in the sun while the porters climb up the mountain. We frequently see swarms of flies buzzing around the meat as the porters pass us on the trail. Simple math said, "Avoid yak meat at all costs!!" Unfortunately, these trekkers either didn't see what we saw or chose to ignore it. Sure enough, in the middle of the night we hear every one of them racing to the bathroom and moaning in pain as they deal with diarrhea and vomiting all night. Unfortunately, our room is right next to the bathroom and we hear it all through those paper-thin tea hut walls – all night long. We are honestly afraid that raw sewage and vomit will seep into our room from the overflowing mess they make in the bathroom.

Regarding acclimatization, while I feel stronger and stronger each day, I notice that Chris has had a lingering cough. As we're about to hit the sack for the night, Chris rolls over and says, "Hey can you hear that?" He rolls over again and indeed I can – despite being on the other side of the room, what I'm hearing is fluid sloshing around in his lungs due to high altitude pulmonary edema. I tell Chris the best thing for him to do is descend the mountain before it gets worse. Chris won't have it; he is determined to fight it and continue the climb. (Note: This is not advised!)

Chris is a tough guy who, during one of his many Sydney-to-Hobart yacht races, got stuck in a massive storm which flipped their team's boat in the middle of the night. After hours battling the elements in total darkness, they managed to be rescued. Talk about mental strength!

So, Chris's rationale is that a little pulmonary edema is not going to get in his way. We agree to monitor it closely and reassess accordingly. I listen carefully throughout the night (over the vomiting and diarrhea of the trekkers!) and continue to do so while we remain at altitude the next 24 hours.

Tuesday April 13, 2004
Altitude: 16,520 feet –> 18,010 feet –> 13,730 feet
Gorak Shep to Kala Patthar to Pheriche *(by way of Gorak Shep (to get the rest of the gear) to Lobuche (for lunch) on the descent)***:**

Today the plan is to summit Kala Patthar with a small summit pack, then descend back to Gorak Shep to round up the gear we left there, and ultimately make our way to Pheriche, where we'll spend the night.

We wake to about 2 inches of snow; a thin blanket that makes everything bright. This is in stark contrast to the dark gray of the Himalayan walls, which are so steep that snow prefers to avalanche down versus stick to the walls. The blue sky begins peering out behind the clouds and remains with us the rest of the day.

At 8:00 am we depart Gorak Shep, arrive at Kala Patthar at 10:00 am, and return to Gorak Shep at 11:00 am. We arrive at Lobuche at 12:45 pm for a quick lunch, then head to Pheriche, arriving at 4:45 pm.

Trekking to Kala Patthar in the snow is a great experience. Seeing the six wild Khumbu Quail on the route is a bonus.

The view from Kala Patthar is absolutely extraordinary, even better than the one from the Everest Base Camp. (*No disrespect to Everest Base Camp, but in comparison it's 1000 feet lower in altitude and tucked into the Khumbu glacier which limits the view a bit.*)

From Kala Patthar you get an incredible and expansive 360-degree view of the all the massive and legendary peaks in the region: Everest, Lhotse, Nuptse, Pumori, etc.

The lodge at Pheriche is immaculate and jam-packed with tourists, many of whom seem to be out of their leagues. A lot of them are really suffering from the physical effort, and more profoundly, the high altitude. Throughout the day and night, we hear rescue helicopters taking tourists with altitude sickness back down the mountain.

By the time we reach Pheriche, Chris' altitude sickness symptoms are completely gone and we're both feeling great and absolutely elated.

Wednesday April 14, 2004
Altitude: 13,730 feet –> 12,550 feet
Pheriche to Tengboche:

We leave Pheriche at 7:55 am. At this point, we're motivated to get back down and home.

Just a couple days ago we had planned to stay the night at Pengboche, but we were moving rapidly on our descent and trekked all the way down to Tengboche. I was excited to spend the afternoon/night at Tengboche as it's a monastery town and we weren't able to visit on the way up as no lodging was available.

We arrive at in Tengboche 10:55 am (earlier than expected) and have a solid lunch of Sherpa vegetarian stew and pasta.

After the big meal, Chris and I walk to a ridge past a trekker's lodge. It has a great view, including an amazing vista of Namche Bazaar and all the mountains towering over the valley we just climbed. As we took the Chukhung Ri/Kongma-La pass route to get out to Base Camp earlier in the trek, we haven't had this perspective of the valley and mountains, and we reflect on how blessed we have been weather-wise during the entire trek.

I take a moment to think about what a great sleep I had last night at Pheriche (13,730 feet). Finally, I feel as though I have fully acclimatized. In fact, I feel stronger and more physically fit with each passing day. Throughout this journey, every day built on the prior days' journey; a slow, methodical acclimatization with several opportunities to climb high and sleep low. I can now say I have spent four days trekking over 17,000 feet, and two of the four hitting over 18,000 feet:

Chukhung Ri - 18,200
Kongma-La Pass – 18,100
Everest Base Camp – 17,600
Kala Patthar – 18,500

After that short day-hike I decide to take a quick nap. My legs are tired from descending the past couple days, and I feel I've earned a little rest and relaxation now that the major altitude is behind us.

I wake to the sounds of long horns blowing. Given that Tengboche is a Tibetan monastery village, we know it must be important. Raj knocks on the door to tell me a High Lama is arriving, and a ceremony will take place in the temple. I quickly grab my camera and some cash for a donation.

There are three Tibetan monks in the beautiful monastery when we arrive. We stick around, and after the throng of tourists thin out, Raj arranges for the highest monk/Lama to perform a brief ceremonial blessing and to place a prayer scarf, known as a Khata, around my neck as a blessing to protect us during our journey in the mountains.

it's very special to receive the blessing and Khata. The paintings in the monastery are stunning (and look like the Tibetan furniture my wife and I bought when we moved to Singapore!)

Thursday April 15, 2004
Altitude: 12,550 feet –> 11,110 feet
Tengboche to Namche Bazaar:

Knowing that we're moving quickly on the descent, we decide that tomorrow we'll skip Thami and head straight down to Lukla. In Namche we tried altering our flight to return earlier, but to no avail — all flights were booked. We'll just spend an extra day relaxing in Kathmandu. So, we concluded the trek and the adventure as follows:

Friday April 16, 2004
Altitude 11,110 feet –> 9,300 feet
Namche Bazaar to Lukla

Saturday April 17, 2004
Altitude: 9,300 feet –> 4,300 feet
Lukla to Kathmandu - free afternoon

Sunday April 18, 2004
Altitude: 4,300 feet
Kathmandu (in the morning), with a Kathmandu Tour in the afternoon

Monday April 19, 2004
Altitude: 4,300 feet –> Sea Level
Kathmandu to Singapore

What a tremendous adventure, in an extraordinary country, with a beautiful culture and amazing people! We're absolutely blessed to have had this experience!

As we were waiting to head back to civilization, we both looked at each other and asked the requisite post-trek question:

"So, which mountain do you want to climb next?!..."

Mount Kilimanjaro was the answer, and I was committed to weaving a charitable campaign into climbing to the roof of Africa.

The Seven Strengths of Summiting | **Mark Santino**

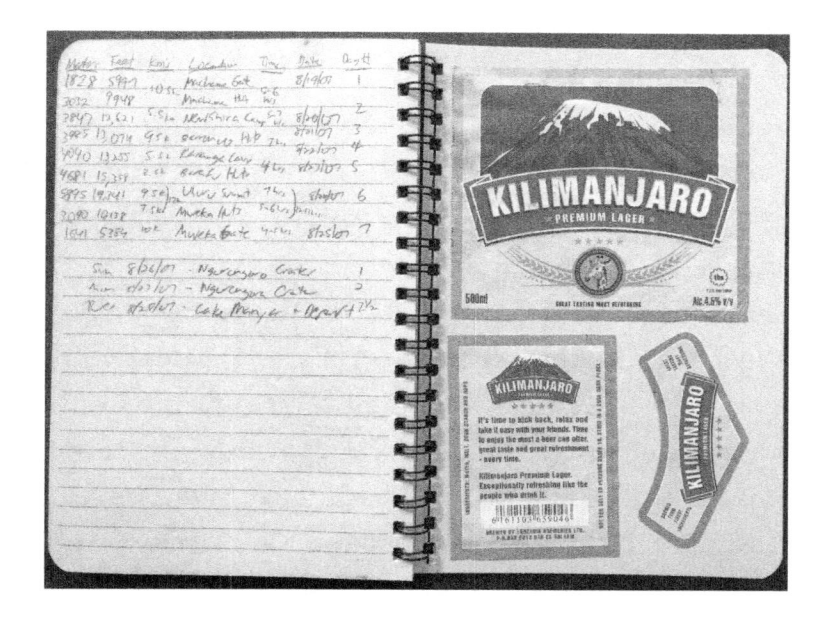

APPENDIX C:
MOUNT KILIMANJARO (2007)

December 16, 2006 – 8:12 am:

"Jambo!" ("Hello!" in Swahili). Welcome to the adventure of a lifetime! It was around Christmas 2006 when I broached the subject of another trek with Ivett. It was closing in on 3 years since the Everest Base Camp (EBC) trek and I wasn't getting any younger or fitter.

Mid-January, I sent out a teaser email to the guys who have been on a few prior treks with me, as well as my hometown buddies. After successfully trekking to Everest Base Camp, as we were descending back into civilization, we vowed the next trek would be Mount Kilimanjaro. I was eager to see who was interested.

Almost as fast as I sent the email out, Cosmin responded with a "Yes!". Cos saw the IMAX Kilimanjaro film and had been thinking about a Kili trek for a few months. More responses came in – fantastic, we've got ourselves a trek! Bruce, James, and Chris were up for the adventure as well.

We took a road trip up north to watch a slide show that Cos discovered about Mount Kilimanjaro. We brought our Kilimanjaro guide books (which I had since the EBC trek), and enjoyed a great slide show presented by an older gentleman who had summited a couple of years earlier.

We discussed the game plan: (1) pick the route, (2) pick the rough dates, (3) pick a guide company, (4) book flights, (5) start training for the big mountain, and (6) make sure our inoculations were up to date. Cos and I quickly did a bunch of research, communicated with the other interested parties, made some quick calls, and by February 1, 2007, we were locked and loaded.

I really wanted to get the date firmed up as I knew I had a lot to do to get fit for this mountain adventure. I had joined a gym a few months earlier, but due to business travel and motivation challenges I hadn't seen much of the gym at all. I knew I would need to get my cardiovascular strength to peak levels. Also, in addition to building overall physical core strength, I knew it would be key to build up leg strength. The sore quads on the descent of EBC, and a tweaked hamstring from the Thanksgiving football game were two hints!

I started searching for a guide company. I reached out to a former co-worker who climbed and unfortunately collapsed on Kili due to altitude sickness a few years back, and my pal Richard, who always seemed to be one mountain ahead of me on our mountain bucket lists. We also began calling guide companies listed in our Kili books. However, once we spoke with the UK Director of IntoAfrica (a fair-trade UK-based HQ and Tanzania-sourced guide company), we knew we had a winner.

August 15, 2007, 2:00 am:

I'm setting the alarm for 3:00 am (an hour from now) to head to the airport! I don't think I slept more than a couple of minutes last night. I was amped — seven months of planning is finally coming to fruition. I should have finished the packing weeks ago. Here I am, itemizing the gear, making photocopies of my travel docs, and re-considering each piece of gear due to the airlines weight limits — instead of getting much needed sleep!

Initial trepidations: Am I fit enough? Acclimatized enough? Will malaria, stomach issues, or diarrhea be a major problem this trek? Will there be geo-political stability issues in Tanzania? Will I make all the travel connections? What about wildlife dangers, as we plan to tent camp in the wild on safari? Will the camera do it all justice? Then there's all the hype… all self-inflicted hype! I've always dreamed of doing a big climb and being sponsored. But months ago, even all the way back to the EBC trek, I was thinking even bigger than that – wouldn't it be awesome to climb for a charity? Absolutely! I'd love to give a little back, as I gain so much from experiencing the culture, the people, the continent and the adventure of a lifetime.

A few months ago, Cos and I were driving across the Central Valley in Northern California, en route to some high-altitude training in Yosemite National Park. Cos has always been up for any adventure: Mount Washington winter ascent; winter snowshoeing/camping up to Bear Mountain (the tallest mountain in Connecticut, which also sits on the Appalachian Trail); plenty of mountain biking across Connecticut; and a quick in-and-out adventure to Yosemite High Country. Besides this trek being a great test for me (sleep deprivation due to the red eye flight, test of altitude and legs after a few months of training at the gym), it would also be a good test for Cos. I took him to the summit of Mount Dana; at over 13,000 feet. It's tough, stressing the lungs and legs and ability to acclimatize, yet it's quick and fun, with incredible views of the region, and he had never been at this altitude before.

Cos fared well. He toughed out a big headache but going from sea level to 13,000 feet in 18 hours is going to do some damage. Definitely cool was that a co-worker Jeff and one of his buddies (also named Jeff) joined us where we hit Vogelsang lake/peak.

On that long drive across Central Valley, Cos and I talked about life, the mountains, politics and everything in between. We shared common perspectives on many topics, which was very cool. It was also a great opportunity to get to know my future Kilimanjaro climbing partner a bit better.

During this car ride, I voiced my desire to climb for a charity. Cos loved the idea. We talked about one day working for a large philanthropic foundation and giving back to the community as a full-time job. I had never run a charitable campaign before, and I really wasn't sure where to start. I thought about two charities where I had volunteered recently as potential beneficiaries for the climb, but I wasn't sure whether either would be compelling enough for folks to want to donate.

Then the lightbulb went off: my employer had a Foundation and a Matching Grants program that would enable the doubling of money if co-workers donated – perfect! After some research and some vetting, we chose the Amani Centre for Street Children in Moshi Tanzania, which takes care of homeless children at the foot of Mount Kilimanjaro. It just seemed right!

We were required to get 10 donors to set up a "Team Event". Could I convince 10 people to donate to a charity they'd never heard of, on a completely different continent? I wasn't sure. The event was called "Mark Santino Climbs Mount Kilimanjaro – Amani Centre for Street Children". My name in lights – which added a bit more performance pressure and anxiety on top of what was already there!

I knew that making the down payment to the guide company for the trek would be instant motivation to train; however, this visible campaign upped the ante big time! Not only am I climbing the mountain for myself, but now (and I can still feel the stress just writing this!) I'm climbing for the kids and others who put their faith and money in me. Our stretch goal at the onset was to raise $3,500 – the cost to take care of 10 kids for one year at Amani (school, food, medical, clothing and counseling). How great would it be to help 10 kids in need?! So, on June 22, 2007, the campaign began.

As the company's Foundation was only for employees, Cosmin initiated his own campaign and a personal (and very generous) matching grant program for those who donated to his campaign. After an amazing level of support, we ended up raising over $5K for the Amani kids! Incredible! That was our super-stretch goal, and we did it in such a short period of time! Wow! Imagine the impact to the kids!!

We arranged to visit Amani while we're in Tanzania where we would meet Valerie, the Executive Director of Amani, who we spoke with during the charity selection process, the Amani staff, and the kids. Should be an eye-opening and very fulfilling experience! What a great way to start our African adventure!

August 16, 2007, 9:52 am:

The tight flight connections are weighing on my mind. I changed my connecting flight to DC a few weeks ago to erase one potential delay, but booking with multiple airlines, switching airlines and terminals, going through customs, weather delays, last-minute gate changes and other variables, I won't be able to relax until we arrive in Tanzania on time.

Parting thoughts as I'm thinking back to Everest Base Camp adventure: There are several elements I feel are critical to be successful in the mountains. They are: (1) Physical Strength, (2) Cardiovascular Strength, (3) Altitudinal Strength, (4) Mental Strength, (5) Spiritual Strength, (6) Family Strength, and (7) Constitutional Strength (the ability to fight off sickness). Mountain trekking adventures are extremely tough. Taking each obstacle one at a time is key. Breaking the big goal down to smaller, manageable goals makes the big goal less daunting, and builds confidence as you successfully achieve each sub-goal.

It also crossed my mind that my interest in climbing Mount Kilimanjaro goes back at least 15 years (~1992) and solidified when I first saw REI's trip offering write-up and read *Travels* by Michael Crichton. Going even further back, my childhood dream of exploring Africa was set when I learned about Stanley and Livingstone's adventures a hundred and fifty years ago. What an amazing opportunity – I feel extremely grateful and blessed!

August 16, 2007:

After finally getting some much-needed rest and food at the airport lounge, I stuff my big daypack into the overhead bin of the airplane, with a number of my critical pieces of gear, including my boots. Admittedly, it's a lot to be lugging around airports and hoping there's overhead bin space on every aircraft, however it's advised to carry on the plane as much of your critical gear as possible. If your luggage is lost or delayed by the airlines, at least you're able to limp by, versus a major trip disruption at best or a trip cancellation at worst). With this, I'm off to Amsterdam for the next connection.

August 17, 2007:

At the crack of dawn, our plane touches down in Amsterdam. I'm a bit worried, as I have to deplane, go through passport control, get my big yellow North Face bag from baggage claim, and go through customs before changing terminals to catch the next flight to Tanzania. Fortunately, it's a very efficient process; I make it through without a hitch and meet Cosmin with plenty of time to spare. We grab something to eat at the Schiphol Cafeteria. The food is reasonably good, and the ham and cheese sandwich really hit the spot.

The plane is delayed upon departure; it sounds like there's a mechanical issue. They eventually sort it out, and still manage to arrive in Tanzania on time.

August 17, 2007, 8:00 pm:

We touch down in Tanzania. How amazing – I'm in Africa! The lines for passport control are long and slow, but "pole pole" (*slowly, slowly*) is the motto of our climb, so it's all good. We pick up our luggage and meet Emmy and her colleague from IntoAfrica. Suddenly, the power goes out. Brief panic sets in as we wonder what could possibly be happening – a million scenarios run through our minds. Fortunately, it only lasts a few minutes, but it's eye-opening that indeed we're not in the big city any longer.

We wait by the van while Emmy sorts out another client's luggage issue. It's cool seeing all these old Land Rovers and Land Cruisers, knowing that they will all be heading out on safari soon.

Before leaving the US, I treated the clothes I was wearing with Permethone, but as soon as I hop into the van, I start fumbling around my day pack for DEET, as I see a couple mosquitos buzzing around inside!

We drive for about an hour through the dark, mostly unlit streets. The roads appear to be fairly well-paved, with the SUV climbing over huge speed bumps as we pass through the villages along the way. Just a few men can be seen walking the streets at night through the villages. As we hit Arusha, we turn off onto an unpaved road and bounce along for what seems like an eternity. Clearly, Emmy knows the road well as she navigates up the rugged drive.

We are greeted by one of the guesthouse's employees holding two glasses of fresh juice on a tray. We are shown our room, which is in a very nice part of the Boma Guest House. We are then asked to come upstairs for our first Chagga meal (the local cuisine). It's quite tasty, and Cos and I have our first Kilimanjaro Beer. To top off the meal, we enjoyed some fried locally grown bananas for dessert. It was delicious.

After a quick shower, I pull down the mosquito net over the bed. It's a little disconcerting to see that that the nets have a few holes in them. In fact, Cos's net already has a handful of Band-Aids covering some of its many holes. I end up not having a great sleep, as the outside lights were blazing through the partially covered windows, and I found myself listening for attacking mosquitos all night.

August 18, 2007:

We speak with Valerie about meeting up at Amani Centre for Street Children, but logistically it looks like it won't work before the climb. The children are going on a safari into Tarangire National Park, and we have to be back in Arusha by 7:00 pm for dinner and the pre-climb meeting. We come to agreement that we'll meet the staff and kids after we descend Mount Kilimanjaro in a few days.

With this change, we join a bunch of tourists from New Zealand and Brian, our trekking partner, for a day in Arusha. The tour pace is slower than expected. We visit the Natural History Museum and the old German Boma (military fort/ living quarters) which is part of the complex as well. We stop for a moment and listen to a wedding band rehearsing – they're great!

We eat a quick lunch at a place called the Crossroads, which is full of locals eating Tanzanian cuisine (i.e. *not* a tourist trap) which was cool. I decide to go easy on the food, as I'm leery about how my stomach will react to this new environment, so I just have an omelet with fries and an orange soda. After lunch, we buy SIM cards to minimize the costs of local calls.

Our next stop will be a local market. I'm excited, as world markets are always lively and colorful. All types of grains, fruits, vegetables, meats, housewares, fish, etc. are available. Of course, we check out a couple souvenir shops along the way.

As we get into the van to head back to the guest house, we meet Kirsten from Amsterdam, who is also part of the climbing party. Dinner is served after the group pre-climb meeting (again, with a Mount Kilimanjaro Beer to top it off), and we meet Liz from New

Zealand, another cool member of the team! We eventually head back to the room to pack our climbing packs.

Reflecting further on the pre-climb comments from the guide company team: Emmy is the local IntoAfrica director – she and the company are amazing! IntoAfrica costs somewhat more than the average trekking company, but they are strong advocates for fair wages for porters and guides, and donate funds to the local community, helping those who need it most and building schools for the children.

Emmy was very emotional as she told us that her people, the Chagga, see the mountain as holy, and she prayed for us to have a safe and successful trek. Simply awesome!

We do some packing to make things a little easier come morning, then hit the sack.

The plan:

Day	Date	Meters	Feet	Kilometers	Location	Duration
Start	8/19/07	1,828	5,997		Machame Gate	
1	8/19/07	3,032	9,948	10.5 km	Machame Hut	5-6 hrs
2	8/20/07	3,847	12,621	5.5 km	New Shira Camp	5-7 hrs
3	8/21/07	3,985	13,074	9.5 km	Barranco Hut	7 hrs
4	8/22/07	4,040	13,255	5.5 km	Karanga Camp	4 hrs
5	8/23/07	4,681	15,358	3.5 km	Barafu Hut	7 hrs
6	8/24/07	5,895 –> 3,090	19,341 –> 10,138	9.5 + 7.5 = 17 km	Uhuru Summit to Mweka Hut	7 hrs + 5-6 hrs = 12-13 hrs
7	8/25/07	1,641	5,384	10 km	Mweka Gate	4-5 hrs

Day	Date	Meters	Feet	Kilometers	Location	Duration
8	8/26/07				Ngorongoro Crater	Safari
9	8/27/07				Ngorongoro Crater	Safari
10	8/28/07				Lake Manyara	Safari

August 19, 2007:

Climb day! We wake up early to complete our last-minute packing, have a team breakfast, and then jump into the bus filled with all the guides, porters, cooks, climbers and our gear. The grand total is 21 support staff: 1 lead guide, 2 assistant guides, 1 cook, 1 assistant cook, and 16 porters. Wow — huge crew — it's a bit embarrassing that we need so much staff just to support our climb!

We drive from Arusha to Machame Village, and finally to Machame Gate where the trek will begin. The road scenery brightens up shortly after we leave Arusha. From the highway, we have an amazing view of Mount Kilimanjaro, and we pull over for some pics.

As we get closer and closer to Machame gate, the road winds through tiny villages as we climb higher into the foothills. It's fantastic how green it gets up here. These views look more like Southeast Asia but with banana and coffee farms dotted with little tiny huts where the locals live. The Tanzanian people look so happy — they're always smiling and greet visitors with a warm "Jambo!"

Once we arrive at the gate, the porters and guides begin to evenly divide up the weight to ensure no porter gets overburdened and put in a dangerous spot on the mountain. The amount of gear, food, and cooking supplies is amazing. I briefly meet the porter who will carry my duffle bag containing my sleeping bag, clothing, etc. (i.e.

everything except for what will be my summit pack/day pack.) I ask the guide leader to have the porter carry the duffle bag upside down when carrying it, as the bag's big zipper is on top, which makes it less than 100% waterproof. We take a few minutes to organize our personal gear (expand the trekking poles, apply the sun block and bugspray, put the scree gaiters on, etc.), and then we officially sign in: Name, date, guide, passport #, occupation, age, etc. This process documents who is on the mountain, and acts as sort of a legal release for the National Park.

There are tons of tourists and trekkers; the Formosa Mountain Club (Taiwan) is here with a dozen or two people. They help us take a group photo, and we do the same for them.

Now the climb begins. It officially starts at approximately 6,000 feet. Today is supposed to take us from the Machame Gate through to Machame Hut at 9,948 feet, over a stretch of about 6 miles. This is one of my favorite days of the climb, as we spend the day climbing through the rain forest. It's deep, thick jungle, and the trees and flora are beyond description. So many unique plants look like they are from another world – I take many pictures, as some of these plants can only be found in this one spot on the entire planet, which further adds to the wonder of Kilimanjaro! While it's overcast, much of the day is fairly dry. Then a misty rain gently falls. This pattern of on-and-off rain continues throughout the day and night. My Gore-Tex and spirits hold up and I am in a great mood, saying "Jambo!" and "Asante Sana!" (Thank you!) to all the porters as they pass. It's always amazing how easily porters are able to pass us on the trail with 2X-3X the weight in their packs, without blinking an eye.

We get settled into our tents at Mweka Camp, have a great hot meal, and hit the sack. Cos and I thought we'd have loads of free time, but as we learn today — and every day — we do not.

After we settle in for the night, one of the climbing teams puts their massive tent just inches away from ours. They're up really late into the night, talking for hours. I make the mistake of not putting earplugs in and get zero sleep all night. Then, at the crack of dawn, their porters (especially the one who talks in a low mumbled monotone) started chatting. Apparently, I was snoring and disturbed Cosmin's rest. We learned that others did not sleep well either. I hear that one of the trekkers had never slept in a tent before this trip — talk about trial by fire!

August 20, 2007:

Today starts misty and damp. We're supposed to hike from Mweka Hut to New Shira Camp at 12,621 feet, but the day turns into a butt-kicker. It rains all day long. At midday we stop under a rock ledge for a quick lunch and some relief from the elements. It's not a large rock ledge, but we squeeze as many of the trekkers and porters underneath the overhang, in an attempt to keep everybody dry.

Our lunch is prepared each morning by our cook and stored in a rectangle plasticware container to keep it from getting crushed (and today, dry!). The first couple days I eat almost everything in the lunch container, but then I start getting pickier as time passes; I stop eating the chicken leg as I'm worried about my stomach.

The combination of rain and wind is brutal. The weather and altitude are affecting everyone, and even the most talkative of our trekking party are very quiet today as they mentally battle the elements.

Then the cold sets in. We shiver as we eat. The porters are dramatically underdressed for this type of weather. Heck, it's the dry season and it virtually never rains this time of the year. Most of them are in shorts; many of them wear cotton clothing, and all are shivering and hungry. I give away half my lunch as well as several energy bars, snacks, nuts, etc. that I have in my day pack. As fast as I can dish out food, the porters and guides are eagerly grabbing it. "Asante Sana Mzungu!" ("Thank you very much Mzungu (white man)!"). I wish I could do more, but it feels good to help these guys who are helping us throughout this huge endeavor.

We decide to press on, back into the rain, to get to New Shira Camp. While it's painful getting pelted by cold rain and wind, getting the blood flowing again by moving briskly causes the shivering to stop. After another hour or so of trekking, we make it to the camp, where it continues to rain. We settle into our wet and muddy tents and attempt to find dry clothes to change into.

This is when I learn how bad things are. Despite asking that my duffle bag be carried flipped over to keep the rain out, it had not been. Virtually all my gear was completely soaked, including the clothing I was wearing.

But it gets even worse. All of our porters are soaked, as is all of their personal gear. Our lead guide tells Cos that things are bad, and we may need to head back down the mountain. I'm extremely frustrated to hear that we might have to turn back. And while I understand the reality, I don't feel it's acceptable that the guide company didn't prepare the crew for rain.

We join the team for dinner. Two of our trekkers are beaten down pretty badly by the harsh day and are close to throwing in the towel, but the other two are unfazed. The three of us remain optimistic, trying to keep the others' spirits up.

I'm vocal that we'd been given a very specific, comprehensive gear list from the guide company's Executive Director — not once, but twice. I feel very strongly that insisting the trekkers be prepared for the elements, but not the trekking company's own team, is not just objectionable, but downright dangerous.

Within minutes, Julius comes into the dining tent. He listens to our questions and concerns, and we discuss alternatives. We agreed to spend a second day at New Shira Camp to give the porters a chance to dry out and rest (and hopefully, to give the weather a chance to clear).

We all agree. The new plan is that we'll attempt a day hike to the Lava Tower at 14,600 feet, before returning to New Shira Camp. It will add more miles to the trek and eliminate an intermediate camp (Karanga) but offers a good opportunity for the team to dry out and everyone to acclimatize.

This was a very reasonable alternative. I feel better with an alternative plan that's safe and prudent for the porters and climbers. (*Gear note to self: For next trek, ensure I use more hardcore garbage bags to wrap essential gear, invest in a pack cover, bring more TP and baby wipes, and more clean clothes!*)

In the middle of the night we're awoken abruptly by Kirsten. I think something must be wrong, but it's quite the opposite: She is ecstatic. "Look!" she says as she points upwards towards the night sky. The clouds have parted and, in the darkness with a half-moon now lighting the landscape, we can clearly see Kibu, the top of Mount Kilimanjaro! We haven't been able to catch a glimpse of it since we saw it from the road a few days ago. The sight gives us new hope.

The clearing of the storm clouds and rain brings in cold winds, but I don't mind – cold and dry is far better than rain any day!

One thing I'm struggling with as I reflect on the past 24 hours and the next 24-48 hours is the weather. With the amount of time I've spent in the mountains (and with the use of my altimeter watch's barometric pressure trending functionality), I'm usually pretty good at telling when bad weather is coming or going. This weather was so odd. It was building up from the elevation below and rising to envelop us in wetness and clouds. During the next day there would be a battle between the sun and the clouds from above and the wetness from below; as you read on, you'll see we lose this battle too.

August 21, 2007:

We wake again at New Shira Camp. It's dry now, and everyone is in good spirits. We discuss the plan for the day at breakfast. I hit the "long drop" as I need to urinate before hitting the trail; that's when the diarrhea hits me head on. I race back to my backpack to grab my TP and sprint to a toilet that had a door (not all of them did!). When I finally emerge, Cosmin has orchestrated the entire team of porters, cooks, guides and trekkers to applaud. Embarrassing, to say the least!

Man, what bad news — this diarrhea wrecks me and weakens me all day. After a couple hours of climbing it hits me again, this time next to a rock at 13,500 feet. This really sucks. I decide to start taking the Ciproflaxin and Immodium AD, and I drink a ton to prevent dehydration.

This climb is slow-going. I feel the cool, moist air rising up the mountains from the growing clouds below. The blue sky above us is soon replaced with ominous looking clouds. Once again, it looks like we're between a proverbial rock and a hard place with potentially bad weather about to hit us from all sides.

The only bright spot at that moment is seeing a serval cat (black spotted golden cat with a long tail) that we witness pouncing across the rocks about 100 yards in front of us at 14,000 feet. What an amazing sight! Julius moves quickly in its direction to get a better look, he's in such great shape, the altitude doesn't slow him down at all!

The moist air below us and the clouds above us envelope us again, turning into rain ... until the cold wind kicks in and turns the rain into snow. This mix of rain and snow hammers us until we start to descend. We reach around 14,200 feet, which is good from an acclimatization perspective, but our dry clothes are getting wet again.

So, you're probably wondering, "If all your gear was absolutely soaked yesterday, how did you survive the night?" There's an expression in the mountains: "Cotton Kills". And, fortunately all my clothing and my sleeping bag are synthetic. While it doesn't dry instantly, it will keep you warm when wet. So, all night last night I was up, changing into wet clothes, using my body heat to dry it throughout the night. While I missed the much-needed sleep, through this process I was able to expand my selection of dry clothes from just a couple items, to drying most of the critical clothing and gear elements. Really, it was successful night!

As the rain and snow falls on me today, I grow concerned that all that effort to dry gear last night was just a waste of time. I also feel the same way about our progress on the mountain – here we are at 14,000 feet, now descending and heading backwards on the route to the camp we left this morning. There's an expression that distance in the mountains does not always equal progress. While I understand the value of the acclimatization progress we make today, and why we need a day for the team to rest and dry out, heading down the mountain to New Shira Camp with my bad stomach put me in an irritable mood.

Looking back up at Kibu, the same view now for multiple days, makes me more frustrated than excited. No one want to hear any more bad news. I ask Julius straight up, "What's the plan for tomorrow?" He says with some confidence that we're moving up to Barranco Huts/Camp. This is what I wanted to hear at last! Real progress! We'll attempt to hit Lava Tower at over 15,000 feet on our way back down to Barranco at 13,074 feet.

I call home. While I'm not able to reach anyone, I am able to leave a voicemail message for my wife. In the message I share how bad the weather is. Admittedly, I've been heavily introspective over the past couple of days. I never expected the weather to be such a huge factor, and my optimism is coming and going in waves. Julius says it has NEVER rained this much in August as far back as he can remember. It never crossed my mind that the summit attempt might not even be presented. Also, the diarrhea has made me weaker. Lastly, and most profoundly, I'm shaken by terrible news we learned from the Assistant Guide Godfrey: During yesterday's heavy rain, two porters from another trekking group (two days ahead of us/higher than us on the mountain) had died from exposure. They were both with a local trekking company, which apparently already had a poor reputation for not taking the best care of its porters. Julius later informs us that the Kilimanjaro National Park immediately changed regulations to include not only weight inspections of all porters' bags at the start of the trek, but also a gear inspection of the porters to ensure they can also handle the intensity of the mountains. Extremely sad circumstances, but in the long term it is really good news for the porters and their families. It's shocking that most guide companies don't appear to be doing this audit themselves as part of their standard operating procedures. With the news of these deaths, on top of all the other challenges, emotions are high.

The second course of Cipro and Immodium has slowed down the diarrhea, and I'm starting to feel a little better. I'm finally able to reach my wife, and we speak briefly before the SIM card's minutes run out. I reassure her that we're moving up the mountain tomorrow, and the drugs are making my stomach feel better.

Before night closes in, the formal "Introduction Ceremony" of the porters to the trekkers is held. It's great to put names to their faces, and we really feel a bond due to the hardship of the three days of rain on the mountain.

August 22, 2007:

The plan for today is to climb from New Shira Camp to Barranco Camp, by way of the Lava Tower. Reaching the top of the Lava Tower at 15,200 feet would be great for acclimatization and a good physical push. We keep watching the clouds. It seems a little less threatening than yesterday, but there's still a lot of cloud cover below us. I constantly monitor the clouds, wind, air moisture, air temperature and barometer as we ascend.

After several hours of trekking, we can see in the distance the side trail up to Lava Tower and the Barranco trail intersection. It appears to be about 30-60 minutes away. Julius asks how I feel and whether or not I can go up to Lava Tower. I tell him I'll let him know at the junction, as my stomach is still not feeling great and the weather is still questionable. Pushing forward aggressively to hit Lava Tower, only to get stuck in more rain, was the main factor I was weighing.

As the junction arrives, I look up at the clouds and instinctively say we should proceed to the Lava Tower. This is a good call as climbing high and sleeping low is important from an acclimatization perspective.

After a fairly quick side trip to the Lava Tower and long day of trekking, we make it to the Barranco Camp. While we're only around 13,000 feet, with 6,000+ more feet to the summit, it does feel great that we're no longer at Shira! In fact, we've gone from what felt like zero progress for the past couple of days, to an amazing fact: Tomorrow we'll move from Barranco to Barafu, sleep briefly, and push to the summit!! Yes, the summit attempt will commence tomorrow night! This revelation is exciting and a little scary at the same time. Sleep, which has eluded me all week, will be critical – no pressure!!

August 23, 2007:

Today's trek will take us from Barranco to Barafu at 15,358 feet. It will be a long day. The initial plan was to take two separate days to get through this section. As we lost a day due to the bad storms, we'll have to skip sleeping at Karanga Camp, and just trek through it instead. The upside is that we'll have a hot lunch at Karanga as we pass through it. I relish the idea of a hot lunch, as those cold plasticware lunches are getting a little bit old. While I don't eat everything in those cold lunch containers, the food that I do eat is usually great!

The climb from Barranco requires us to climb the 700-foot Barranco Wall, definitely the most technical climb of the trek. It certainly has a lot of character: We need to scramble up the side of the mountain on a narrow ledge that's near vertical in some spots. I pray that no one gets hurt, especially the porters who'll be weighed down with bulky and awkward packs up this dangerous stretch of the climb.

The weather has been good all day. It seems as though we left the wet and volatile clouds below us, but you never know on a big mountain like Kilimanjaro. As we ascend from Mweka Hut to New Shira Camp, I look on the bright side and keep saying that the rain is good for Tanzania. For all those families we saw getting water from natural wells on our drive up to Machame Gate, in fact, for tens of thousands of people who await the rain for water to drink and to feed their crops during the dry season, this is a godsend. The rain may have given us hell the past several days, but it's a blessing for the dry lands and the communities living at the foot of the mountain.

Ah, today is finally sunny in the high mountain. After trekking all morning through some of the most beautiful (yet rugged) terrain, we arrive at Karanga at lunch time. I hop into our dining tent, which for the first time this week is not dripping wet and muddy. While lunch is being prepared, I take some time to sit and relax in the tent and scribble out a couple pages of notes in my journal. What a nice, long, relaxing lunch. Too bad we're not staying here all day as initially planned, as I'd love to chill out in the warm sun and relax and breathe in the clean mountain air; however, we've got to progress across Karanga Valley to Barafu this afternoon.

We get to Barafu later than expected, around 5:30 pm. The word "Barafu" means ice/snow in Swahili. And while it's neither icy nor snowy here today, it is indeed cooler than it has been so far this trek. The view from the camp and the "tourist toilet" outhouse window view is amazing, with a gorgeous view of Mwenzi Mountain, part of the Kilimanjaro summit peaks. While our site is lower on the mountain versus other camps, it's a good one. Dinner really is excellent tonight! Amongst all the dinner options is pasta, plain wide elbow pasta with butter/oil. I add some salt and eat two huge bowls – carbo loading! This is the first big meal in many days for me, due to my stomach challenges. A few days ago, I cut out the hot tea/coffee/chocolate I was consuming each night, hoping that reducing my caffeine and sugar intake would help me sleep better. I've been just drinking hot water, which is good as well (as long as I don't burn my mouth!)

Tonight, we have to "sleep" from 7:00 pm to 10:00 pm, and wake for a 10:00 pm "Alpine start" up to the summit.

Unfortunately, my mind was racing with excitement and I slept very little. This is going to be one heck of a climb!

The next thing I hear is, "Wake up! We're going to have a quick breakfast before we climb to the Summit". It's 10:00 pm, and we have to load up our summit packs, eat quickly, and begin climbing soon. Elias (the camp assistant) "knocks" on the tent door as he has done every morning "Hello, did you sleep well?" he warmly asks. I can't believe it's finally game time and I don't think I sleep a wink. I hear that Brian hasn't slept at all either; misery loves company, I guess. Last night was a warm night from my perspective. All the guidebooks say climbers need to sleep wearing every ounce of clothing they have on summit night at Barafu due to extreme cold, but I found last night to be a bit warm. I guess I'm a hot sleeper.

I quickly organize and load up the last essentials of the summit pack, have a quick bite, and brace myself for the big day. We hit the trail at 11:30 pm. We must be one of the first teams to begin the ascent. Most folks get up at midnight to start climbing at 1:00 am or later, while we started our "day" two hours earlier.

As we pass through the upper Barafu camps, it's still pretty dark and quiet. Julius begins singing a Swahili song; its soothing melody helps us get into to a rhythm for the climb. The Tanzanian style of trekking is "pole pole" (*slowly, slowly*). The pace is much slower that I'm used to, but I know going slowly is critical to acclimatization. In the days preceding summit night, I was struggling to get into this rhythm. I was more used to my 4-to-8 breath pace with an incorporated rest step. This was out of sync with Julius' rhythm and apparently was a little frustrating for folks the past few days.

On summit night I'm doing my own thing: deep breathing and the 4-to-8 breath pace. The deep breathing approach made Julius and the assistant guides nervous all week, as they thought I was having trouble breathing. In general, when I trek there's a good 10-20 feet between me and the next trekker, so no one really hears how I breathe to acclimatize. With the pole-pole style, "I step where you just stepped" and you're very close to the trekker right in front of you, watching their feet versus the view around you. While I struggle a bit getting used to this approach, I'm fully acclimatized. No headache, no stomachache, no dizziness, no nothing. Just feeling strong and enjoying breathing in the thin, crisp, clean, mountain air!

August 24, 2007, 1:30 am:

This night is long and hard. As we gain elevation rapidly, a trail of headlamps stretches up to the sky as far as we can see – and straight below us as well. I made the mistake of not changing my head lamp batteries before the trek began. The light is so dim, that I just turn it off. This ends up being an added challenge.

Exhaustion – not the muscular kind, but raw fatigue due to lack of sleep – kicks in early. I keep moving, one foot in front of the other, but I'm drained. I call out (in jest) looking for a coffee or an energy drink! I give in and do the "Pole-Pole/I-Step-In-Your-Step" routine. I do it because if I slow to look up/down or do a rest step, Julius calls out "Mark, are you okay?" I don't want to fall behind, or worse, "get pulled." And I definitely don't want to be the subject of the Lead

Guide's attention, so I just follow step. I do, however, misstep a few times due to being so tired. Several times I just plant my trekking poles and close my eyes for a couple seconds. I feel my body "close its eyes" too, and I begin to wobble. I say to myself, "Holy crap, I'm falling asleep standing up!" just like you see in the cartoons! To counter, I breathe in deeper, and stomp when I plant each foot. I need to get the blood flowing and wake up.

The mental pressure of not wanting to "get pulled" from the privilege of climbing is enough to keep me moving forward and staying awake. The altitude is a non-issue; my legs are strong, but I'm tired after the mere 30 minutes of sleep I got earlier this evening.

Julius was clear with me that I was moving too slowly. He said, "Stop here. Don't question me." I'm thinking, "oh no, this is it – he's going to pull me from the climb". However, when I stop, he removes the two water bottles attached to my summit pack. That's about a half-gallon of water weighing around 4 pounds. It's incredible, what a huge difference 4 pounds makes. I have a total of 5 liters of water with me; in retrospect, it's too much. Cutting corners on water is risky; however, for this specific summit night it's a non-issue, and it's helping me a ton to be relieved of this weight. Julius and Godfrey will each carrying one of my bottles to the top of the mountain for me. I'm really glad Julius stopped me, and I immediately begin moving at a healthy pace.

Suddenly, Brian stops, saying he feels terrible – light-headed, bad headache, feels like vomiting – the works. The assistant guide, GodBless, takes Brian's pack and falls behind us on the trail. I figure that's it; that Brian is heading down. I feel bad – I know how badly he wants to achieve this goal. He suffered all week, but powered through the hardship each day, and it's a shame to see him fall back.

And then it was just the four of us. Cosmin calls out that my pole-pole-step-style is messing up his cadence, and he moves ahead of me, just behind Julius in line. As we get closer to the top, I notice that Cos is all over the place; stepping wildly to the left and to the right. The altitude just hit him like a ton of bricks. He falls to the back of the line as best I could tell.

Godfrey then yells out the time "4:19 am!" It's bad news and good news. Bad news: while it's a couple hours to daylight, we're still several hours to the summit. Good news: we've been making really good progress — moving fast, with virtually no breaks, except for a couple occasions of adding or removing layers as we warm up or cool down. I opted to wear my Himalayan mitts for gloves. While they're extremely warm and toasty, with mitts you lose all dexterity and you need to be completely reliant on others to help with things as simple as getting water, or you'll be constantly take the mitts off and freeze your hands (or risk dropping a mitt and the wind taking it down the mountain). Being this reliant, this high on the mountain, is dangerous and I won't do it again.

So, it was a couple hours to daylight. I started thinking, yes, I'm tired, but what I really need is the light to wake up my brain. I'm sure that when daylight hits, not only will it warm up this frigid air, but it'll wake up my mind and body and give me that extra boost I need for the summit.

When I turned off that headlamp earlier, not only was I mis-stepping more, but the darkness added to my sleepiness. Light will be the solution, and I resolve to get the headlamp fired back up right away.

Easier said than done! Without a headlamp and having these big bulky mitts on, I was a mess trying to find the replacement batteries. I finally found them, and with Julius' help, got them installed in the headlamp. The beam is bright – really bright – it's giving me the added boost I need!

The next hour is the toughest. While the headlamp helps, I'm still extraordinarily sleepy. Just as I happen to glance up at the horizon, I see this very fine, thin band of light across the sky. It appears as one layer of green on top a thin layer of red cutting across the pitch-black sky. "Yes - sunlight is coming! I can do this!" The wind is blowing, it's getting colder and colder. Everyone is freezing. I had taken my Gore-Tex pants off a couple hours earlier when I was overheating, climbing in soft shell pants which were windproof. I had taken off my Gore-Tex jacket too; however, I put it back on again. With that adjustment, my temperature is dialed back in. The soft-shell pants, soft-shell gloves (which I had on for a little bit before I put the big mitts on), and wind stopper jacket are awesome. They're bombproof and fight off the cold and windy extremes well, while regulating heat.

We push and push higher on the mountain. Suddenly, Julius announces, "We're here at Stella Point!"

"What? We're here already? How is that possible?" Incredible – the toughest part of the climb is behind us! We gather by a large rock. I take a couple photos of the ragged crew. And within minutes, that green and red band is growing redder, then red-orange, and then a ball of orange which begins to light up the whole sky. Morning is here!

Conversation at the summit is a joke; I'm incapable of getting a clear sentence out due to lack of sleep.

Kirsten, Liz and I are the first three to reach Stella Point with Julius, our lead guide. A few minutes later Cosmin approaches. His face is white as a ghost, and his eyes are failing to focus. He looks like he's had 15 beers, stumbling everywhere. I immediately say, "You need to descend now." This was cerebral edema in black and white. My intent was not to undermine the Lead Guide's authority. Julius said the night before, "only I can tell you that you can turn around", so the guides can continue to motivate the clients high on the mountain when a little encouragement from the guides might be all it takes to achieve their goal. Of course, it's Julius's call, but I am worried for my friend. Julius turns to Cosmin and asks, "What do you think?" Cosmin says, "One more try".

This section between Stella Point (18,871 feet) and Uhuru Summit (19,341 feet) is extremely icy and slick due to wet weather the past several days and freezing over at this high elevation. Cosmin slides all over the place and can barely stay vertical while just trying to take those couple steps. He is a danger to himself and others (flailing trekking poles are weapons!). We quickly take a few photos and Cosmin heads down the mountain with Godfrey. With cerebral edema, rapid descent is the only real solution.

It seems like only a matter of seconds after Cosmin's departure when Brian and the assistant guide GodBless arrive. We all thought Brian had descended back down to camp; instead, he was pressing forward, fighting the same battles we were to get to this point. I look at the timestamp from the picture I took when Kirsten, Liz and I arrived, and only 15 minutes had passed. Brian stays for a moment for a photo; apparently GodBless asks him, "Summit?" and Brian instinctively says, "Yes" and keeps moving up the mountain. As we fumble around with water and clothing adjustments, snapping photos, and assessing Cosmin's condition, Brian departs, heading up to the summit. Before Cosmin descended, I heard him ask whether we (at Stella Point) were higher than Everest Base Camp. I looked down at my altimeter watch and said, "Yes, indeed we are!" I glance over at Kirsten, who has had a bad cough all week as she made the summit climb. Her lips are blue – a clear sign of oxygen deprivation – but she's a trouper and is ready to move up to the summit. Off we go to Uhuru, the ultimate summit of Kilimanjaro.

  Seeing other trekkers on the mountain is scary and funny at the same time. It looks like everyone is in battle with that "thousand-yard, glazed over stare." We had seen so many lights on the way up, but there are so few people here. "Where did they all go?", we wonder. Julius reckons that most turned back down the mountain. Wow! Statistics about what percentage of people actually summit Mount Kilimanjaro are hard to find. Clearly, most don't make it based on what we're seeing (or should I say, did *not* see) at the Summit. The extra 500 feet from Stella Point to the Uhuru true summit is slow-going due to ice and tired legs.

  About 20 minutes after seeing Brian and GodBless zip past us heading down, we reach the Uhuru summit. Finally, Kirsten, Liz, Julius and I stand on the Roof of Africa: Mount Kilimanjaro! We take some quick pictures as we wait for our turn to take a photo in front of the famous sign at the summit. The wind is bitter cold, and Julius is eager to get back down the mountain. We take our photos and start our descent.

Now, not only do we have to head back down to Barafu, where we had our brief base camp sleep less than 12 hours ago, but we have to pack up everything there and descend all the way down to Mweka Huts/Camp: a massive 9,200 feet descent, TODAY!

The scree descent is a nightmare. This is how accidents happen: altitude, tired muscles, exhaustion, and loose dirt and rocks. We learn from Cos that he was so bad off from the cerebral edema, he slid all the way down the scree on his butt, tearing up his Gore-Tex pants and his bottom side. Kirsten's knee is killing her. Julius takes her pack, and she descend very slowly. I go slowly, too; my legs are tired and getting more tired with every second as I try to protect my knees by breaking with my quads.

Finally, Barafu High Camp is within sight. I ask, in a moment of weakness, if Julius can carry my pack too. At this stage, my quads are quivering and I'm moving at a snail's pace. I'm embarrassed, but he agrees, and I'm able to regain my strength and move more quickly down the mountain.

As we get closer to the high camp and the grade of the decent lessens, I ask Julius for my backpack. He asks if I can carry Kirsten's pack instead, and I agree immediately. He helped me when I needed it most, and now it's my turn to help him.

Note: I'd like to comment that this "Alpine Start" is not my favorite, especially after zero sleep, for obvious reasons. I like seeing what I'm climbing from a visual experience perspective, but also a safety perspective: to avoid hazards on the ascent and know where you've been if a rapid decent is needed. But "Alpine Starts" are imperative to (1) get to the summit before the afternoon weather volatility hits, and (2) have the time to summit and return to base camp, pack up everything and get to the evening's camp while daylight.

Finally, we stumble into camp. Every porter from every trekking party along the camp says, "Congratulations!" After the long night of climbing and pain of descending, it's nice to reflect, "Yah, we did it!"

We're instructed to rest for only an hour, after which we'll grab a quick hot lunch and begin the descent to Mweka Huts. That one hour is awesome. It goes by in a blink, but it recharges our batteries. After lunch we began the descent which will take another 3½ hours, but we learn it will be a good descent on a proper non-scree trail!

Slowly watching the altimeter "unwind", we finally stroll into Mweka Huts camp. Wow — what chaos! There are hundreds of tents everywhere. After checking in, we have a long walk through what seems like a mile of tents until we reach our campsite. I wonder how the heck they found the campsite with all the tents strewn about the massive camp!

It was an incredible day: about 18 hours of trekking, over 11 miles, with 4,000 feet vertical elevation gain to the highest peak on the continent, followed by a 9,000-foot descent. We feel super-human!

What comes next is truly a dinner for kings. All our meal favorites are here, including Ugali, a local Chagga specialty. We discuss our logistics around tipping the crew, try to freshen up a little bit and then, mercifully, hit the sack.

August 25, 2007:

We all sleep like babies, for the first time in over a week. Man, that felt great! Today we undertake the final descent off the mountain from Mweka Huts at 10,138 feet to Mweka Gate at 5,384 feet; a nearly 5,000-foot descent.

Before descending, we hold the "tipping ceremony". We (the trekkers) agreed on an amount for the support team's gratuity the prior evening and Liz plays the role of the banker, making sure each guide, assistant guide, cook, assistant cook, and porter gets their fair and appropriate tip. These tips are our way of expressing gratitude to the whole team for their essential work on the mountain. They did an absolutely incredible job!

After the tipping ceremony, the porters and whole team sing the "Kilimanjaro-Kilimanjaro" song. This the high point of the entire trek! It's great seeing the whole group sing from their hearts and sway to the celebratory song!

When the song ends, they pack up camp and literally race down the mountain. We joke, "Pole Pole!" as they run past us with their massive packs. They're eager to pick up their paychecks, which are customarily paid in cash at the Exit Gate, and to get home to their families after a long, hard, and brutally wet and cold week.

Mweka Huts camp, which we just left, is a very green camp, and as we descend, we traverse through deep rain forest, similar to Day 1 of our climb. It's a great climate zone to be descending through; we're told that there are five zones on Kilimanjaro, ranging from the cultivated zone, to the rain forest zone, to the alpine zone on the mountain, and everything in between.

The Seven Strengths of Summiting | **Mark Santino**

My eyes open wide to observe nature at its finest and we really have a chance to take it all in now that the difficult part is behind us. The bearded lichen hanging from the trees, the unique flowers, the cut logs lining the trail that have literally sprung back to life with full sprouts growing upwards out of the logs towards the sky, and ancient trees still standing tall because the land is protected. Shades and shades of green – just fantastic!

Brian and I chat most of the way out as we reflect upon this adventure to the roof of Africa. We both agree that the teamwork with the guide company and all the trekkers was incredible, and really helped us get all to the top of the mountain. Everyone gave selflessly to make sure we were in the best shape for a challenging week. What a great team!

We finally make it to Mweka Gate, where we wait patiently to get our official Kilimanjaro Summit Certificate as proof of our successful climb. A few local kids offer to scrub muddy boots for a small fee, and when we see the great job they do, we take them up on their offer. It feels very civilized to have clean boots for the flight back home.

We walk through many tiny villages from the gate back to the parking area where our van is waiting. Beautiful banana and coffee plants line yards and small huts.

We end up at up at a little tiny village restaurant where we eat "Chris-burgers" (hamburgers topped with a fried egg) in a box. Delicious! After eating, we board the big van which ferries the whole crew of nearly 30 of us back to Arusha. Various porters hop out at stops along the way to head home. At one of these stops, Cosmin, Rosy, and jump out and met Athman, who will be our driver to the Amani Centre for Street Children in Moshi.

The last entry in my journal listed the whole IntoAfrica team. These guys were exceptionally warm and wonderful people and did an extraordinary job, battling adversity with the extreme rain and cold, and getting us to the summit and back safely. We can't thank you enough! Thank you: Julius (Lead Guide), Godfrey (Assistant Guide), GodBless (Assistant Guide), Eodger (Cook), Emanual (Cook), Idd Porter), Goodwork (Porter), Elias (Porter), Salemantt (Porter), Sansa Porter), Kennedy (Porter), Omary (Porter), Omary-Mallid (Porter), Aniseth (Porter), George (Porter), Willy (Porter), Edward (Porter), Frank Porter), Enarist (Porter), Richard (Porter), Loshibicki (Porter), Henry Safari Guide), Athman (Driver on Safari and Moshi), Emanual (Safari Cook), Emmy (Tanzania Director), Rosy (Tanzania Assistant Director), and Chris (UK Director)!

"So, which mountain do you want to climb next?!..."

The Seven Strengths of Summiting | **Mark Santino**

ABOUT THE AUTHOR

Mark Santino enjoys adventure travel, mountain biking, Brazilian Jiu Jitsu, and challenging himself on mountaintops around the world. While Mark has summited Mount Kilimanjaro and trekked to Mount Everest Base Camp, he especially enjoys immersing himself in other cultures while exploring some of the most beautiful places on the planet, regardless of altitude. When each adventure ends, Mark is happy to rejoin his wife Ivett, daughter Nicole, and son Joey at their home in northeastern United States.

Notable Mountains:

- First big mountain I trekked to the top of was near Tucson, Arizona: Mount Wrightson @ 9,453 feet in 1992 (including a high-altitude mountain lion encounter!) The other peaks in the Tucson area include Mount Lemmon @ 9,080 feet, and Rincon Peak @ 8,482 feet.

- Mount Lassen @ 10,463 feet in Northern California – first peak I felt the effects of altitude sickness in the form of a pounding headache.

- Mount Dana @ 13,061 feet in Northern California – first peak over 13,000 feet; I've done this hike multiple times – it's a great challenging climb and the view is amazing. Mount Hoffman @ 10,856 feet in California. Clouds Rest @ 9,931 feet and Half Dome @ 8,839 feet in California.

- My next big mountain was Mount Whitney in Southern California, the tallest mountain in the continental U.S. @ 14,496 feet in 1997.

- My first mountaineering ascent with crampons, ice axe, and ropes was to the top of Mount Shasta @ 14,180 feet in 1998.

- Highest peak on the Australian continent: Mount Kosciuszko @ 7,310 feet in 2003.

- Highest peak in Japan: Mount Fuji @ 12,388 feet in 2003.

- In Nepal's Himalayas: Mount Everest Base Camp @ 17,600 feet, Kala Patthar @ 18,514 feet, Chukhung Ri @ 18,196 feet in 2004.

- Highest peak in Africa: Mount Kilimanjaro @ 19,341 feet in 2007.
- Machu Picchu and Inca Trail via the Salcantay Route @ 15,200 feet in 2009.
- Patagonia National Park in Chile & Argentina in 2014.
- The Haute Route 100 miles trek in the Alps from Mont Blanc (Chamonix, France) to the Matterhorn (Zermatt, Switzerland) in 2019.
- Hiking, backpacking, and exploring numerous U.S. National Parks over the years (Yosemite, Yellowstone, Glacier, Sequoia, Kings Canyon, Acadia, Grand Canyon, Zion, Arches, Canyonlands, Saguaro, Bryce Canyon, Capitol Reef, Everglades, Grand Teton, Haleakala, Lassen Volcanic, Petrified Forest, Pinnacles, etc.)
- New England Peaks climbed Mount Washington @ 6,289 feet including winter ascent, and Mount Katahdin @ 5,269 feet including its precipitous Knife Edge route.

The Seven Strengths of Summiting | **Mark Santino**

Printed in Great Britain
by Amazon